Echoes of a Whisper

Carlton Brown Harvey

Published by CBH Products
Atlanta, Georgia
www.cbhproducts.com

Discuss the book @
www.facebook.com/echoesofawhisper

Get to know the author @ www.facebook.com/cbh314

Copyright 2010 by Carlton Brown Harvey

Published by CBH Products
Atlanta, Georgia
www.cbhproducts.com

ISBN 978-1463788827

Printed in the United States of America

Contents

Echoes of a Whisper

*Many souls speak well
but few souls speak worth.*

He steps out and closes the car door, slowly giving the place the once over. He can't imagine that the person he is looking for could very well be in this breakfast restaurant. But his friend recommended that he checked out this Waffle House around three to four in the morning during the middle of the week and guaranteed he would find the man he was seeking. He's now questioning the validity behind his friend's words but he's here, so might as well walk in at the very least.

Upon entering he looks over the ten people seated inside. There are a couple of groups of friends hanging out late night and two workers behind the counter talking to the patrons as if to be good friends that go way back. He looks across to the far end of the building and finds a man sitting alone. The waiter has just brought the customer his food which consists of three strips of bacon, a waffle, two slices of toasted bread, a bowl of grits with melted butter over top and two eggs over well. It is a meal fit for a king.

The guest decides to walk over to this gentleman since he is the only patron sitting alone and the only one who seems to hold the slightest possibility of being the soul he is seeking. He walks over hesitantly and speaks softly at first.

"Ex...excuse me sir, I do not mean to bother you in the middle of your meal but I have been looking for someone and I was wondering if you might be him?" The gentleman looks up from his glass of orange juice that he has just taken a sip from and smiles at the guest before responding to his statement.

"Well I guess that depends on who you are seeking." The guest smiles and nods slightly. This gentleman seems to be a friendly fellow with an inviting demeanor.

"Well I have a friend who told me I might find someone here that I have been searching for the past few weeks. He's supposed to be a wise man but I find it hard to believe that a wise man would be found in an establishment such as this." The seated gentleman smiles and chuckles a bit. He then encourages his guest to rest off of his feet.

"Have a seat, my friend, get comfortable. Would you like something to eat?"

"Well uh no, it's 3:16 in the morning. I generally do not eat breakfast at this time of night. It's a little late, don't you think?"

"Oh well it's never too early or late to eat breakfast, my friend. You should try something from the menu."

"Well uh no, I really don't feel like it."

"Well would you in the very least like something to drink? I don't want to be sitting here eating this meal in front of you while you sit there empty handed."

"Okay, I can get something to drink. What do you suggest?"

"Hmm, well water or sweet tea is always a winner for me."

"I don't drink sweet tea."

"Hmm, must not be from around here. Well then, how 'bout you try the vanilla coke, that's good stuff too."

"Well, all right, it's worth a try." A worker comes over and brings the guest a glass of vanilla coke and also refills the gentleman's orange juice. The guest takes a sip of the coke.

"Mmm, you're right, this is good."

"You trust in me when it comes to Waffle House; I won't lead you astray." The gentleman pauses for a moment and then readdresses the meaning behind the guest's visit. "So, a wise man you seek, correct?"

"Right, may you be him?"

"Well, I don't know about wise but maybe I can address some of your concerns."

"Like I said before, I find it difficult to believe that a wise man could be found in an establishment such as this."

"What? Would you expect one to be found in a high, snow-covered mountain far off in a distant land, meditating in a cave atop a flight of a thousand stairs?"

"Well-yeah I guess or at least not in a breakfast restaurant in the middle of the night."

"Hmm, well wise men must eat too, don't you think? Besides, it's not where you are on the outside that makes you wise; it's where you are on the inside. Hmm, mentioning that reminds me of a story I was once told, about the fool and the straggler."

"The fool and the straggler?"

"Yeah, a fool was once hastily straightening and cleaning up his house because he was told that a wise man was coming to visit. A tattered straggler happened to enter the home unannounced and came to the fool. The stranger asked this soul to keep him company and join in good conversation. The fool dismissed the straggler and told him that he was too busy making preparations to properly receive a wise man. The straggler was saddened by the fool's response but accepted his answer humbly. Needless to say, the fool never met the wise man.

"What interest does a wise soul have in the appearance of your house? It's the content of your heart that concerns such a soul. It is your internal appearance that should be valued most, not your external. But most souls know these things, yet and still, it is difficult to keep them in mind." The guest eyes widen just a bit as he has now caught his first glimpse of this soul that he has sought. "So who are you that you would search for a wise man?"

"Well, my friend says I am a fool who needs a little guidance. He was the one who told me that I was searching for something. I'm a bit skeptical of his half-baked analysis of my disposition but I decided to entertain his assertion none the less. Entertaining my friend's thoughts have brought me here to a Waffle House at three in the morning. So once again I ask, do you think you may possibly be that wise soul to whom my friend was referring?"

"I am more comfortable with the term lover than wise soul."

"Lover?"

"Yes, but not in the way that you are familiar with." The gentleman pauses for a moment while he takes a couple of bites from his bacon and toast. After washing it down with some orange juice he continues. "I've found there to be many kinds of souls in this world, five of which are the fools, the settlers, the seekers, the lovers and the authentic souls. I consider myself a lover."

"What does that mean?"

"Well, quite simply, it means that I am in love. I'm in love with something which, right now, is beyond my comprehension. I just recently became a lover, before, I was a seeker. Meaning, I was searching for something, not knowing what it was or could be but I searched looking for an answer to a question. It was difficult because along with the answer, I didn't know the question. But one day my heart became pricked by the answer, like catching the faint scent of a lost lover traveling on a summer's breeze. This scent, this tugging at the heart, gave me my question and my answer. So now I am a lover, returning to the Love I once knew. A voyager traveling back Home."

"And where is Home, what is that Love?"

"Mmm, only the authentics know, only the authentic souls have found that answer. I would be blessed to come across an authentic one day, truly blessed. But in my ignorance I refer to it as the Eternal."

"So with our brief encounter what would you deem me? Am I a fool, maybe a settler?"

"Possibly a fool but not a settler. A fool does not seek at all and they believe they know what they truly do not. A wise soul recognizes what he knows and acknowledges that he knows it. A wise soul also recognizes what he does not know and acknowledges that he does not know it. A fool fails to do these two things, generally erring on the second condition.

"You could possibly be a fool but you are not a settler. A settler finds an answer, though it may not be true, and holds tight to it. The settler never sways or challenges what he believes he knows. A bit stubborn but at least they have something to make them feel secure. The only difference between a fool and a settler is that at least the settler recognized that there was something to be sought after but the fool is too knowledgeable to have to seek for anything.

"You have sought me out so you could possibly be a seeker. Seekers do not search to find what believers believe; they yearn to know what the knowers know. Time will tell which type you are but keep in mind, souls are not static and the classifications are not distinct. They overlap mightily. There are days when even I act a fool but my heart always drifts back to being a lover. That is who I am."

"A lover sounds overly romantic to me."

"Don't get it confused, I am a lover but I am no fool. I see life clearly; I understand the rules of the game. That is what makes an authentic soul, authentic. They possess a depth and clarity in their sight that unveils the world in truth, not perception. They are the knowers and I would hope to come across one of them someday. In the very least, I wish to find another lover who has been pricked in the way I have so I may not have to travel alone. A group would be best but one would suffice. True lovers seem to be a rare commodity in this world."

"So how did you come to the point of being a lover, besides being pricked? What text did you follow while you were a seeker?"

"After a time of searching I found that what I sought for could not be held complete in text alone. Simply reading scriptures is like reading the directions on a map without ever traveling to the destination. Why spend so much time quoting and standing on scripture alone? They alone will never enable you to reach or touch the Eternal. Words are the foundation but do not confuse them with the apex. All authentic souls do not merely recite scripture, they speak from the knowledge of themselves because they have traveled the road themselves."

"So are you saying religious texts are not needed? Are you saying that souls can do without them?"

"No, they are useful to those who need guidance and direction. They have been passed down through the centuries for a purpose that is not vain. But take note, if every religious text was wiped off the planet overnight, we would still possess all that is needed to find Home. The Truth has been written upon the hearts of all souls and that is Love. So when it comes to texts, you'd do well in not mistaking the map for the destination. Text can become a prison to those who seek the Eternal if they are not applied insightfully."

"And how do you know when a text is being applied insightfully? How do you know when you are or are not in error?"

"Do not be a settler; continue challenging what you know or what you think you know. Continue to search and do not be satisfied. Continue to think because you were given a mind for that reason so you should put it to good use. A restless and unsatisfied thinker can travel far provided that soul never settles. That soul will see many sights and pass through many lands because he is always eager to see more and search deeper. That soul will touch frontiers yet to be known by the world.

"If I had to choose between a soul that possessed a library's worth of knowledge and a thinker, I would choose the thinker every time. Anyone can gather knowledge but a thinker discovers things yet to be known. Remember, it is not what you know but your ability to apply the knowledge you already possess. Thinkers go out and attain the knowledge relevant to themselves."

"You sound a bit like a preacher."

"Maybe but I recognize that I have to wipe my own feet before I step in the house. Men are still men. Allow those who can assist you to assist you but only follow the Eternal. It is difficult for a soul that is served by many to keep their focus on returning Home. There is nothing evil about being a leader in the world, provided you remain a servant to the One. What greater service is there in the world than to serve the One? A soul that serves the Eternal possesses more power in serving that One than ruling trillions."

"If an authentic soul willed it, how many souls could they command?"

"An authentic could command legions of souls without a word being spoken."

"How is it possible to lead without taking action?"

"The same way a tree grows up to embrace the light of the sun. The same way water travels up, against the force of gravity, from the roots in the ground into the leaves on the branches of a tree. It is in the nature of an authentic soul to compel without apparent effort. Take note, it is souls that rule without command who are of the highest power and it is souls that bow the lowest who are the very foundation of existence.

"Always remember what it means to be a servant. A fool says 'I will do this, this and this for the Eternal.' But a wise man asks, 'Eternal, what will you have me do for you?' Wise and authentic souls do not over step their mark or impose their own will. They remain attentive to the soft voice within their hearts and strain not to be haughty or think too highly of themselves.

"One time there was a hardy fool who was strutting and stomping across the ground expressing his superiority over the land. The fool then looked down toward the ground and began to brag, 'Ha, ground, don't you wish you could be like me? I am able to step on you and across you at will. I constantly use you to achieve my own goals. I spit on you whenever I want, I kick up your dirt, I dig into you and fill you with holes. Tell me ground, how much do you envy me? Don't you wish you were born in my position, over you?'

"The ground, irritated by the fool's arrogant rant, began to shake violently. The ground caused a fierce quake that shook the fool to his knees. The fool began to crawl along the ground begging it to stop. The fool was flat on his stomach clinching to the ground before the quake ceased. The ground then spoke, 'It is true, you can stand and walk upon me without second thought to my existence but take note: without me, everything that you are will fall.' The souls that bow the lowest are the foundation of existence; these are the souls that I would like to be in company with. I would love to spend my life with souls that are close to me on the path back Home; I wish to spend my days with the lovers."

They both sit and pause for a moment as the wise soul eats a spoonful of his grits and pours a bit more syrup over his waffles. He looks up at his guest who appears to be deep in thought. The wise soul speaks.

"Okay, I really cannot have you sitting here without a plate in front of you. Do you like hash browns?"

"Well, I'm not sure I..." The wise soul turns to one of the workers and calls out an order.

"Cheryl, could you bring my friend here an order of hash browns?" He turns to his guest and asks, "Do you like onions?"

"Uh, yeah I guess." The wise soul turns back to Cheryl.

"Mak'em scattered, smoothered and covered, and put it on my tab if you would please." The waitress turns to respond.

"Sure thing hun, is that all?"

"Yes ma'am, 'preciate it." As the wise soul gets back to his meal, his guest continues the conversation.

"What are lovers like? You seem to be enamored with them, besides being one yourself, what is their appeal to you?"

"Like you just noted, their main appeal to me is that they are souls like me. They reflect my essence, they reflect my nature, they reflect everything I enjoy being. Lovers possess minds that are fluid, hearts that are open, feet that are willing and eyes that are searching. They are souls unafraid of standing naked before a crowd of a thousand. These are souls that are very beautiful to me. They yearn to be fulfilled, the same as I do."

"Standing naked before a crowd of a thousand? That sounds a bit perverse to me."

"I mean that figuratively but if you would like to take it literally then let's speak on it. If nudity it self was perverse then why were Adam and Eve created without clothes? If nudity was disgraceful then wouldn't humans have been born with something to wear upon birth? When the Eternal is unveiled to humans, is the Eternal not laid bare before us? Isn't that what it means to be unveiled? What perversity is there in nudity besides that which you project upon it?

"If you are inspired to call a naked body degrading and degenerate then that spirit comes from you not the object viewed. That is a statement which reflects the condition of your own heart and not the condition of nudity.

"I see beauty in nudity, so who am I? What spirit do I possess? Let me explain, if anything were to distract and keep you separate from the Eternal then you are deviant and should stay clear of it. If you love your spouse of marriage more than you love and seek the Eternal then you, my friend, are sinful. But do not dwell on condemnation. Soon enough, your heart will realize what it is missing and it'll correct its own ways."

"So what do you think of sin? Is there truly no evil in the world?"

"I try not to focus on the quality of good or evil. I remain a traveler on a path set for Home. When I stray from that path, it is sin. Oh my, my, my how I have sinned and continue to sin. But to return to the path is to ask for forgiveness, there are no verbal apologies. Words do not always reflect the alliance of the heart. And to be forgiven is to be embraced by the Eternal, which is to come back to life. In unity there is life but separation is death. Besides that, good and evil are of no concern to me."

"What of all the pain and suffering in the world? Are they not evil or is that a part of our subjective opinion of the natural and unnatural disasters that occur in our lives?"

"The pain comes from separation, just like death comes from ignorance. If we knew the Source, such pain would pass away."

"So you say that if all souls knew the Eternal then peace would reign and natural disasters would cease to occur?"

"No, simply that natural disasters do not bother the wise and peace between humans is not what the wise seek. The wise seek peace within themselves. Once this brand of peace has been achieved within all then peace between each other will come about naturally, of due course."

"Idealistic, if you ask me. I do not believe such peace could ever be accomplished in this world."

"Yes, long and narrow is the path but the authentic endure."

"You truly are a romantic. You seem to completely ignore the human condition and human nature. We are not always commendable creatures. We often can be very disgusting in our appearance and behavior. We truly can be degenerate dark hearted souls. But even in the presence of such disdaining attributes you resist recognizing good and evil?"

"Not only do I resist focusing on good and evil but I also know that we are the Eternal reflected in human form. I've heard of men who have murdered; I've heard of men who have committed mass genocide against their neighbors. I've known of souls that enjoy terrorizing and torturing others. I've heard the stories of cannibals who eat fellow humans. I've known souls who are detestable rapist and even souls who neglect all of their duties and are attuned to their own sensual desires. But what does any of this matter to me? How do any of these observances detract from the assertions I have made? Your focus remains on the coarse exterior of the pail, when it needs to turn to the essential water of life that is carried within." The guest sitting with the gentleman is not yet satisfied with the wise soul's response but the soul has more to say.

"When others saw a mountain top covered with trees and foliage, the mind's eye of Borglum and Robinson saw the faces of four presidential leaders that now rest on the side of Mount Rushmore. When other souls could only identify a dirty old marble slab of rock and a blank ceiling, the perceptive eye of Michelangelo saw the figure of a young David, and God reaching out to Adam in the Sistine Chapel. This is how the eye of a wise man perceives the heart of all souls.

"When others can only see a coarse rocklike exterior, covered with mold and grime, the wise soul sees the light of the Divine glowing deep at the heart's core. Because even the wise man has acts of atrocities in his past. But like Michelangelo, through lifetimes of sculpting, he has chipped away at the rock exterior until the crystalized form of the heart has been reached. At this point, the wise soul begins to polish the heart until it becomes clear and transparent to the soul's eye. Once this is accomplished, the wise man concentrates on the core of the heart until his eye has become cultured and keen in its perception. It is at this moment the soul becomes true and sees the light that shines within us all, even the killers and tyrants. The heart only needs to be attended to and sculpted, to become a work of divine art, the highest art that exists.

"If you would like to find evil in the world and label it as such, then you can, if you feel it is necessary. If you feel it is your duty then go out and condemn the world. But as you are preoccupied with your search for evil, you'll be neglecting your search for Home."

The guest is taken back by the words of the wise soul. He takes time to think about his statement, while the wise soul continues to work on his meal. After a minute's pause the guest comes up with another issue he would like addressed.

"So it is the heart we need to focus on when attempting to become wise souls. It is the heart that needs to become cultured and brought to light. But then what of the law, what is its place in all of this? You refuse to recognize good and evil so what use is the law to tell you the difference between good and evil?" The wise soul finishes consuming his last waffle bite and drinks a bit of orange juice to clear his throat before speaking.

"I told you, what you consider sin or evil is merely a soul walking away from the path. You should think of it no more than that. Now how do you think the path was originally carved? Whom do you believe blazed the original trail? It was wise souls that walked in accordance with the law. The law is an important aspect of the path; it gives it definition. If you keep to it then you are sure to eventually reach Home, where Love resides. To walk away from the path is like disobeying the law. Allow me to relay a story another lover once told me while I remained a seeker.

"Two fools once crossed paths with a wise man. The wise man had a blissful smile on his face, a smile unlike any they had ever seen. They approached the wise man and asked, 'What makes you smile in such a manner?' The wise man responded, 'I have seen the Garden of Paradise and since then, I have not been disturbed.' The fools asked for the location of the Garden so that they may know peace like the wise man. This is what the wise man told them, 'Do you see that path there? Follow that path and listen to your heart, and there is no doubt that you shall discover Paradise.' The fools decided to heed the words of the wise man and they began their trek together on the path.

"They walked for quite some ways down the path when one of the fools stopped. The second fool also halted to ask the first, 'Why have you stopped?' 'My heart speaks to me.' 'What does it say?' 'To leave the path and walk through these woods.' The second fool scoffed at the other fools comment and encouraged him to believe that he was being deceived by his heart. The second fool said that they both should stay on the path because they are sure to reach the Garden by following it. The disturbed fool then explained that his heart has been speaking to him for some time now but he had previously been able to resist its pull. Now, the burden had become so heavy that he must trek into the wilderness, for better or worse, because his heart has spoken to him.

"The second fool tried to restrain the first fool and they began to wrestle on the path. Eventually, the first fool was able to escape the grasp of the second and said, 'Did not the wise soul tell us to follow the path AND listen to our hearts? But yet you compel me to become deaf.' The second fool reprimanded the first fool and finally left him to his ways. The first fool traveled into the wilderness and the second fool continued on the path.

"After years and years of trekking the path alone, the second fool finally reached the gates of Paradise. Overcome with joy, he knelt down and wept for having persevered through all those years of walking the path. Then he looked closer into the Garden and saw a familiar face. Without hesitation, he ran to the figure and confirmed his initial impression, it was the first fool that had listened to his heart. The second fool asked, 'How long have you been here?' 'An eternity.' 'How did you get here so quickly?' 'When I listened to my heart and walked through the wilderness, I saw the edge of Paradise on the horizon. But the journey was painful in reaching the Garden. On the way, I fell into the pit of despair, where I had to cross the torrent of temptation and then, I fought the demons of doubt. I lost my way on many occasions and suffered in ways no soul should ever suffer, but I stayed attuned to the call. All these scars across my body are the mementoes of my struggles but the end proved to be far greater than the means to reach Paradise.' The fools became wise men then celebrated for having reached the place of Eternal bliss, where they rejoiced in the company of the Eternal."

"So it was the soul that disobeyed the law that reached Paradise first?"

"No, it was the soul that listened to his heart, who reached Paradise first. But you saw what he went through as a result of abandoning the path. This soul would have truly been lost if it were not for his determined will to continue to follow his heart without falling prey to the darkness around him.

"Most avoid that which tempts them, in fear they will not be able to resist its allure. But there are those who are able to walk right past that which tempts them and not give it a second thought. The superior horse is the one which walks straight without blinders. But it takes a very mature soul to rely on such a method of returning Home."

"So you are saying that the greater soul is the one that is able to walk away from the path and still reach Home?"

"Please do not look at it that way, it is truly misleading. There is an obvious distinction between souls-those who walk by the definition of the law and those that carry the spirit of the law within their own hearts. Which is better? Neither. They are different but the same. For if a child does not know better, it is best for it to follow the instructions of its parents without question. But a time comes when a child will challenge the old laws of its youth to test the validity of these laws and come to understanding. This is the disturbance of adolescence, when the youth openly challenges the traditions of antiquity, only to find the truth of the spirit hidden within the wisdom of its parents' instructions. This is the moment the child becomes an adult and honors the beauty of its parents' wisdom and guidance. This is a soul that now carries the spirit of wisdom within its own heart. This is a soul that commits right action and avoids wrong action not in a conscious effort to follow the written law but of due course, led by the inclinations of its own pure heart. This is a soul that is close to peace. You see, a righteous soul is not recognized by its ability to abstain from sinful acts but being devoid of the desire in the first place, now that is a virtuous soul."

"That seems impossible. How could you possibly rid yourself of the desires of your own heart?"

"By rediscovering that which your heart truly desires. There is a saying that goes, 'Deny them what they want and they'll crave it for a lifetime; give them what they want and they'll grow tired of it and resume searching for what they do want.' There are times when it is easier to hold back the wind than act against the desires of your own heart. The heart must be disciplined so when you act righteously it is not simply just that, an act."

"Your teachings seem dangerous. A soul could easily become lost following what you say."

"That is why you must listen to your heart AND follow the path. There are times in which lovers say, 'I don't understand myself. I contradict myself in every motion I make but yet, the path I tread is straight.' These words are so true if you have ever been a lover and when you are a lover, to you, it all seems to make sense. An easy way to keep a seeker from falling is to not push the bird out of its nest before it is ready to fly and who but the Mother knows when its child is ready to fly?"

The guest takes note of the wise soul's demeanor. During the whole of the conversation he seems very relaxed and calm, almost as if nothing in the world could faze him. It is like nothing in the world would knock him off of his stride. This observation leads the guest to another statement.

"Based on the words you've spoken earlier, you do not seem to hold unexpected disasters as reasons for disturbance. Is there anything that could happen in life which would truly bring heartache to your soul? Do you not even fear your own death?"

"It has been a while since I truly feared death. I fear ignorance but not death. What is the use of being preoccupied with something that is inevitable? When death comes, let it come. For now, I am concerned with life. Truly I say, death is the easy part, it's thinking of death that scares you. To me the when, why, how, where and under what circumstances I die, are simply the cosmetics on the face of death. Quit with your preoccupation, quit with your fear because in the end, life moves on no matter what."

"So you are saying that if you were in a life threatening accident and it was up to a doctor to save your life, you would treat that moment with complete apathy?"

"Show me the man who has saved someone's life and I'll show you the man who has merely postponed death. The dead cannot offer life. Only that which is alive can offer life. Apathy, no, but I do realize death waits for us all. I am more concerned with the dead that are living."

"Okay, now you're starting to lose me."

"I've already told you, unity is life, separation is death."

"Separation from what?"

"Home, separation from Love. What else have we been talking about this whole time?"

Their conversation is interrupted as Cheryl brings the hash browns to the table. They look good and the guest cannot wait to dig in as the wise soul hands him a bottle of ketchup.

"Thank you, Cheryl, I didn't want my friend here to leave on an empty stomach."

"It's no problem at all, it just gives me something to do as I wait until my shift is up."

"When you off?"

"Seven."

"Oh, so you got a little while?"

"Yeah, a little less than three hours but what makes it worse is that I've been having these back spasms for the past week or so. I can hardly stand on my feet for any extended length of time."

"Is that right?"

"Yeah, I don't know what is causing it but this past week

has been absolute hell." The guest takes a break from his plate of hash browns, in which he has already put a good size dent, to comment on Cheryl's last statement.

"You know, you shouldn't complain so much, there are others in the world who suffer much worse than you do."

"How, in anyway, is knowing the pain of others supposed to relieve me of my own pain?"

"It isn't, I just spoke as a gesture, to give you some perspective on your own pain in comparison to others."

"What perspective have you given me, besides that we are a race of sufferers?" The wise soul begins to chuckle under his breath.

"I'm sorry I just thought I would say."

"Well now you have, thank you very much." Cheryl turns to the wise soul. "I'll see you again soon, I'm sure."

"More than likely, it was good seeing you."

"You too hun, I hope y'all enjoy your meal." Cheryl walks back behind the counter and the guest speaks up.

"I was just trying to help give her some perspective."

"Obviously you failed in that regard. It'd probably have been better if you offered her some painkillers instead of perspective." The wise man gives a rye smirk to his guest, who is now watching a group of patrons pay their bills and leave. He takes note of some of the food they have left on the table.

"Look at that, look at all the food they've left on their plates. What a waste! Someone could have made good use of that."

"Maybe you should go over there and finish it for them."

"Now why would I do that?"

"Because then it would not be wasted."

"No, you're missing my point."

"Well, then please enlighten me." The wise man is now speaking in a sarcastic tone.

"Are you not concerned with those that are starving across the world? Do you not care about them at all?"

"I do care but I fail to see how finishing that plate of food will end starvation. Then again, I fail to see how if everyone on the planet had three hardy meals a day, that would end starvation."

"Excuse me?"

"Never mind, I'm talking over your head again. I simply mean to relay that I seek the substance which sustains all life. You know, one time I was speaking with another friend, not unlike yourself, sharing the same philosophies on life.

"I found him crying and so I inquired about the cause of his dismay. He said, 'At the age of five I lost my right leg and was forced to use crutches. At seven I lost my other leg and was forced into a wheelchair. At eleven I lost the use of my arms so that I have no limbs. And now I am beginning to lose my sight and hearing. What an unfortunate life I've led. And soon my body will be over taken by a cureless disease.' I sat quietly for a moment as the tears continued to stream down my friend's face. Having collected my thoughts I then asked, 'Is that all you've lost?' My friend responded, 'What else is there for me to lose?' I then broke out in tears and began crying along with my friend. As you may very well imagine, at this point, my friend became perplexed and asked, 'Why did you only begin crying after my response to your final question?' I then said, 'Because in all your hardship, you do not even recognize your greatest loss.'" The guest of the wise soul is thrown a bit off by this tale.

"I must say that I'm not sure if you are wise but you truly sound odd." The wise soul laughs at this comment.

"I have been called such on more than one occasion. Here, allow me to relay another story to you and see if it does not tickle your heart.

"A fool and a wise man were once gazing at a most peculiar site, a trailer sitting beside a mansion. The wise man paused for a moment and then asked the fool, 'Which home do you think is more valuable the mansion or the trailer?' The fool scoffed and laughed at the wise man's question and answered hardily, 'And you call me a fool? Well of course, the mansion is more valuable.' The wise man smiled and they both went on their way.

"During the week a front of storms moved through the area and many tornadoes touched down. The storms ravaged and destroyed the mansion, leveling it to the ground, while the trailer was tossed and thrown a mile away from its original location. The wise man and the fool returned to the same spot a week later and witnessed the results of the storm. The wise man then looked toward the fool and said, 'It seems that Nature does not hold the same sentiment as you. She destroyed both the mansion and the trailer with equal worth.'" At the conclusion of this tale the guest begins to laugh.

"That was unique. I enjoyed that one."

"Yes but did you understand it?"

"I did, I did. It tickled my heart as you said." The wise soul smiles.

"That's a term lovers use in reference to hearing words of wisdom or witnessing acts of Love. But lovers know that the greatest words are those left unspoken and inaudible to the ears. These are the words that speak softly to the heart and rouse the Great Action. I tell you that silence speaks volumes. My own ignorance becomes manifested every time I speak.

"There are those who can fluently speak several different languages but my only concern is with speaking One. But it is a language I'll continue speaking long after my body has perished. I wonder how many souls can, in truth, say that?"

"Do you have any more words that would tickle the heart?"

"Hmm, yes I may very well have words that would tease your ear. A wise man once came across a fool staring at a speck of dirt on his finger. The wise man watched the fool for a short time and when his presence was not acknowledged he spoke to the fool. 'Hello, what are you doing?' The fool answered, 'I'm staring at this speck on my finger. Do you see it? Is it not the most beautiful sight you've ever seen?' The wise man looked curiously at the fool and then turned to look at the vast beauty in the world around them. The wise man spoke again, 'Well, if you would only look around you'll realize that there is much more beauty to behold. All around you is a world of miracles waiting to be discovered.' The fool then said, 'If I look away from this speck it may get blown away by the wind and be lost forever. I do not want to lose it, this speck is mine and I'll never let it go.' The wise man replied, 'I see, you sound very attached. In that case, I'll leave you here clinging to your speck.' The things we cherish in life appear so foolish once we've gained the proper perspective." The guest then twitches a bit as he feels his heart tremble.

"I think I'm beginning to see now why you call certain souls lovers."

"I'll assume that is a good thing."

"Yes, a very good thing." The guest pauses for a moment while he takes another sip of his vanilla coke. "So tell me, do you meditate, do you read scripture and practice the rituals of religious traditions? You seem like the type soul that would but upon speaking with you and hearing your words, I'm not so sure."

"That is definitely a question worth asking. I do all of those things but not in the manner you may be accustomed."

"As I expected."

"I write, that is what I do. And through writing, I worship in a way that is truly personal and special to me."

"What do you write?"

"The story. The same story that every soul is writing in their own way and in their own style. It is this story that I believe in and it is this story that'll lead me Home."

"And what of those that meditate and do the other things that I have mentioned?"

"I do them too, just in the method offered to me. The Eternal provided me with an apple, which is my story. The one who meditates was given grapes, the scripture reader has an orange, and the ritualist holds a melon. Our fruits are different but yet, we've all been provided with more than enough to sustain us on the path Home. As long as your rituals bring you closer to the Eternal, do not cease them. But once your bread has gone stale will you not look to cultivate another batch? The Eternal does not seek to conform you. Love allows you to be who you are, knowing that who you are is fulfilled within the Eternal. And when it comes to ritual offerings, if you're going to give, give from your heart not out of obligation or moral gratification. And if you're going to give, give something worth possessing. Start by giving Love, the rest is found of due course. Because we already know, those that seek...."

"...shall find."

"Yes so when they say today is the day of worship and rest, smile and think to yourself, 'Is not every day a day of worship for those who know the Eternal? Every day I rest in the arms of the Comforter.' And do not think yourself a fool for that. Wherever you find the Eternal, go to that place, do that thing, be that person. In all things be your self, for Love is not far. Seek Love, do not always be caught up with the world.

"I say there was once a fool who was admiring the prowess of two grand armies. Upon observing their might in battle he said, 'Look at those two great armies battling. Such power, what majesty, has there ever been a conflict greater than this one? Which side do you believe the Eternal is with?

Which does the Eternal support?' A wise man standing near by responded, 'At this point, neither side is with the Eternal, they are too focused on each other to spend anytime seeking Home. I would hope that one side completely wipes out the other so then at least one group could return to seeking the Eternal'. The fool then responded, 'No but then that one group would create divisions within it self and continue the battle'. The wise man sighed and murmured, 'Alas, the plight of humanity, perceiving differences where none exist'.

"With the same sentiment, do not waste your time arguing with a fool, unless you wish to become a fool yourself." After hearing these words the guest was compelled to ask this of the wise soul.

"Who are you?"

"I'm you in disguise."

"So who are we? What is a soul? What is our relation to the Eternal? What is our relation to each other?"

"Souls are the echoes of a whisper. We are the breath which gives the dirt life. And what is life but purpose? Souls are like snowflakes that have fallen from heaven. No two are identical but they all fall from the same cloud. Their only hope is to themselves, melt away so that they may return to that cloud."

"That sounds beautiful, very beautiful indeed but is it true?"

"Even Yoda knew that 'luminous beings are we, not this crude matter.' How can a puppet know what a man does not? I am not the skin that clothes me and I run deeper than the blood that courses through my veins. I am not the personality I display; I am simply the sum of that spiritual equation."

"What more is there?"

"To return Home and become what we once were. How can the body survive with a cancer living inside of it? It cannot. The body must separate its self from that cancer. But what if you are the cancer, what then? How can you separate yourself from yourself? There is only one means of that, dying unto your self and embracing the reality you once were. Because lovers should dream of Love and not themselves in Love."

"What does that even mean?"

"It means that souls are the dust of stars reflecting the light of eternity. And what is that light but Truth. So if one is to ask you 'what are souls?' tell them that we are the stars shedding our light unto the world."

"And our light is Eternal."

"That is Truth."

"So in Truth, we are the Home that we search for, the Love that we seek."

"It is written upon our hearts."

"But how do you know that, how could you prove what you say is Truth?"

"It is foolish trying to prove either that the Eternal exists or does not exist. Foolish because it is logically impossible. I've never heard an argument that proved Love's existence nor have I heard an argument that disproved Love's existence. That is like proving the existence of light to a blind soul. How would you go about performing such a task? How could you share light with those incapable of detecting it? All I know is that when Love comes upon you, you know it and your acts become the proof of Love. You do not argue for the existence of Love, you simply experience it."

"What of miracles? A miracle would prove this fact."

"What miracle could be performed which would prove the Eternal? What miracle could be performed that science would not one day explain? What we call miracles are simply events, in the world, that are rare and unusual in their appearance. They in no way prove the existence of a supernatural being. Miracles simply prove the existence of a rare and unusual phenomenon that has yet to be understood. If your eyes were not so lazy you would wake up and look around you. Then you would witness the miraculous occurring in every moment of life. But souls, being lazy as we are, look for signs instead of Truth. Signs have become our truth. But if it is a miracle you would like to witness then I'll tell you one to seek. The greatest miracle to be witnessed is when a lost child finally finds its way Home. No miracle is greater than that."

"So, within us eternity abides and through an authentic soul a dream is realized; all power and knowledge rest with such a soul and there's no more for that soul to do."

"Yes, but you must understand this aspect of life. When it comes to power, the world looks for an aggressive awe-inspiring display of a mighty force. They only see the Eternal like a flood rushing over and washing away all enemies without resistance. Or they perceive the Eternal like an explosive and destructive volcano which extinguishes all life around it. But I say that the true show of Love's power is even more subtle than that. Love's will is done unbeknownst to all enemies.

"The power of the Eternal is like the flow of trickling water which carved out the grandest of canyons. The Eternal moves softly and does not always voice or boast its strength with an omnipotent exhibition of force and violence. The fool laughs at water. The fool says that he can take up water and consume it at will. The fool says that he can disperse water so it loses its form and vanishes, but water is never lost and water is never destroyed. But what the fool fails to realize is that even he cannot live without water. So who is the more powerful, the fool that believes he is manipulating the water or the water that sustains the life of the fool?

"This expresses the omnipotent power of the Eternal. The Eternal moves and expresses its self but no one takes notice. Love's will is being carved into the hearts of all souls like the river of that grand canyon. The will carves into the stone exterior of the heart until it has reached its core and then, revealed is the power of Love. Revealed is the light that shines brighter than the sun. Even now, the omnipotent power of the Eternal flows through me but like trickling water, you will not realize its effect until the will is complete. Until you realize the truth, you are still an ignorant fool wielding a sword of impotence. And if you believe that your sword can cut down the will of Love then slice away, cut through it and see if the water does not still remain."

"And what of knowledge?"

"I'll relay what a wise soul once told me when I asked the same question.

"I don't even know how many hairs are on the top of my head nor do I know the number of stars in the sky. But how does this take away from the knowledge I possess? Allow me to explain. A fool once approached the hand of the body with a question. The fool asked the hand 'How is it that the feet are able to walk?' The hand looked at the fool confused, and responded, 'How do I know? What worth is it for me to know how the feet walk? I am here to do my job which is to take hold of objects, not to grasp that kind of knowledge. But if you want an answer to your question then go to the feet. They know their job better than I should.'

"The fool went to the feet and asked them the same question and this was their response, 'We do not know how we are capable of walking. The brain simply commands us to walk and so without question, we walk. If you would like to know the answer to your question, maybe you should go to the brain, it knows far more than us.'

"The fool then followed the advice of the feet and traveled up to the brain and asked the same question for a third time, hoping for a definite answer. The brain took short time in answering the fool's question because the brain had much work to do. 'I do not know how the feet are capable of walking, I simply know that it is their job and it is my job to direct them. I do not question how I am capable of doing what I do,

I simply fulfill the task I was created to do. I know only what is necessary for me to know, what use is there of knowing trivial knowledge that does not apply to my personal task? If you would like an answer to your question then maybe you should seek the Creator yourself and then even you will find what you have been looking for all along.'"

"So I see."

"Do you now, young soul?"

"I believe I do."

"Allow me to recite one more story for good measure. When I was young, the Eternal gave me a seed and told me to plant and care for it all my life because through this seed the Eternal would provide all that I would ever need. I planted the seed and cared for it and it grew into a beautiful tree.

"One day, fruit ripened and fell from the tree into my hands. I ate the fruit and found a seed within it. I took the seed, planted it and the cycle was repeated. Now many fruits fall daily in my life and I never go hungry because from one seed a forest now stands.

"So, though I may not fully understand its ways, I trust the Eternal with sustaining me. I trust that by providing me with one seed, the Eternal has given everything I could ever possibly want and need in life but note, the Eternal also displays trust in me. The Eternal trusted me not to be lazy so I may work and care for that one seed given to me. My gift expands to the limits of my own responsibility.

"Life is our opportunity to grow, spiritually. It is our chance to aspire to more than that which we have inherited upon being born into the world. Make the most of this opportunity because you never know when it may come again. Seek growth, power and knowledge in life so that you may become a virtuous soul.

"We are ever changing and we are continuously growing. We may not seem the same as yesterday nor do we appear to be tomorrow what we are today but in essential ways we are the same. It is like the day my mother found me laughing. The next day my mother found me crying. The following day my mother found me enraged and even an hour after that, my mother found me asleep. And when I woke, my mother looked into my eyes and called me by name. A lover's ways seem to contradict themselves but they always remain a lover at heart."

"Always a lover, huh?"

"Until I become authentic, yes. But even authentics are lovers at heart because they realize they are Love. Lovers are the dreamers who do not allow their dreams to become passing thoughts. If never acted upon, what else is a dream but a passing thought? Lovers reach out for Love, not in seeking its rewards but simply for Love's sake. They pray without ceasing because no matter what they are saying or doing their hearts remain attentive to the soft whisper within. Because lovers understand the reason they were given hearts in the first place and that is so they may rediscover themselves. For lovers the world is like a playground but they never mistake it for Home. Because lovers know that, 'The world is mine, when I wake up.'"

"That sounds familiar."

"It is a verse from Erykah Badu."

The guest smiles and shakes his head, "How did you become so wise?"

"I sought out the fountain of youth and when I found it I proceeded to drink until I was satisfied-I am still thirsty. That is what I have personally done, if you consider me wise."

"I say you should be proud of your knowledge. I say you should be proud of who you are, you seem very authentic, you seem very true, to me." Upon hearing this, the wise soul spoke his next words in a humble and meek tone.

"Who but Love alone, is authentic and true? I just wish for souls to leave me be and allow me to find my own way. If I could, I'd rather not speak another word for the rest of my life. In truth, I would love to simply dance and sing from now until the day my eyes are finally closed." The wise soul raises his head and his guest nods in agreement.

"Yes, I would wish the same." The wise soul then stands to his feet.

"If you would excuse me but it is almost five."

"Oh yes, yes go right ahead. I didn't mean to keep you for so long." The guest stands up beside the wise soul to embrace him before his departure.

"It is okay, I just hope I gave you a little taste of whatever it is you are seeking."

"You have given me that and so much more. And thank you for the meal, thank you for both meals."

"My pleasure." The wise soul pauses for a moment and looks into the eyes of his guest. "You're no fool, that much I can tell you. Never be satisfied and always be mindful of your heart. If you do these two things then there is no doubt that you will find what you seek."

"Thank you, your words have been a blessing to my soul." The wise soul smiles before departing. He leaves the guest to contemplate all that has been said during this early morning conversation at the Waffle House.

Of Her

Though I do not forsake her body,
I cherish undressing her soul:
this woman of quality, woman of
substance, a treasure to behold.

End of Eternity

"Maybe one day we'll find ourselves to be two halves of the same universe." These were the final words he heard from her before making the conscious decision to forget she ever existed. Because sometimes the only way to forgive someone is to forget they ever were, to forget the life you shared, to forget that piece of yourself.

In truth, there was nothing to be forgiven, this had to happen or at least that's what he kept telling himself. That is the only consolation love lost ever offers, the idea that this *had to happen*. Because true love is supposed to last forever, right? So if love ends, it had to end as if the fate of such souls were truly written in the stars by the hand of an unseen Author. And so it was with them.

But in all honesty, who knows what brought them to this point? Who knows what brought them sitting here at the end of eternity? When a love such as theirs is lost, one only prays to forget such a love ever existed. And then the prayer is made to never again become so committed to something so frail and mortal as love.

At least one of his prayers was answered; forget he did...forget they both did. As for his second prayer, it was not meant to be. Though he does not yet understand what it means, he is a lover and for lovers there *is* a destiny waiting for them written in the stars and etched upon their hearts. So no matter where he runs, no matter how far he travels, there his destiny will be waiting for him to become the lover he was always meant to be.

Appalachia

I've never been a soul well versed in the art of love, but there was one, and I had the fortunate misfortune of falling for her. Appalachia, an appearance matched only by the beauty of her name. Her presence was like that of a summer's breeze; cool, calm, refreshing to be around. She lived her life like a graceful dancer, always light on her feet. It was no wonder why men fell over themselves when falling for her.

I first caught sight of Appalachia by the river, the body of a goddess wading in the water. The surface came just above her chest as she approached in my direction. As not to seem perverse, I kept my eyes focused on the features above water, particularly making sure to look casually into her eyes. But there could be nothing casual about looking at her.

Her eyes were disarming, the type a man could fall into for days. And even now, as she approached, I'd lost track of time. I'd lost track of the minutes between my first sight of her and the moment I realized she was upon me, wading in the river only a few feet away. I'd lost track of the instant she had emerged from the water. I'd lost track of the second I realized the only articles of clothing she had brought to the river, that day, were the ones still lying on the bank by my side, and because of that, I'd lost track of the first words she spoke to me.

"...excuse me?"

"*I said* are you going to sit there and marvel at my architecture or hand me my clothes?"

And with those words I had fallen. I had fallen for a girl who stood bare before me, unassuming in posture, inviting in expression, displaying no signs of apprehension, and wearing a smile that made it all seem en vogue. But it was more than that; she was more than that.

Appalachia was a free soul living an untamed life. She was not one to settle or be controlled. She possessed no attachments and this detachment attracted all to her. She did not seek others to fulfill her; she fulfilled herself. Appalachia did not cling nor would she have you linger. You could not hold her; there was no possessing her. She never allowed another soul to become her world; Appalachia always defined herself. You may come into her life and leave again, but it is you that is enriched by her presence and it is you that is deprived by her absence. Forgive me if my descriptions seem excessive but as hard as I try, words fall just short of Appalachia.

Appalachia opened my heart like a faucet, inspiring verses to run from my pen like water. Her love flowed in and out of my soul, soothing me, revitalizing me and then leaving me whet for more. Ours was not a love of desperation; it was complimentary. For this moment in time was ours, the expression of our love became an art form and when we were together our hearts danced.

"Let us get lost in each other's dreams. That may sound overly romantic but let me be honest, nothing lasts forever so while we have the time let's spend it wisely." Appalachia once spoke those words to me...how prophetic they would become; how indicative they were of our love. For no matter how sweet the dreams we dream, we all must eventually wake up. And the morning I finally awoke still rests fresh upon my mind.

Appalachia had brought me to the river for a swim. On the banks I watched as she slowly undressed, before me, allowing the water to become her only attire. She turned toward me, with an innocence in her eyes not even a child could capture and then called for me to join her. I took a step into the water; a crisp chill came over me at that moment.

But this chill was not a sensation inspired by my feet but by my ears as I heard Appalachia say...

"Take them off."

"Excuse me?"

"You do not want your clothes to get wet, take them off."

"But then I'll be naked."

"And what am I?"

"But you are different, what if someone sees me?"

"Then blessed they would be for having seen you in Truth." I became hesitant; I could not proceed. I could not find the courage to never mind my nudity. "If you are willing to join me then undress yourself and let us travel down this river, together, into the Ocean."

"The Ocean?"

"The origin of all love; the destination of all love."

"I cannot. I would be ashamed."

"What shame is there, besides that which you carry within your own heart?" I'd never heard such words; I'd never heard a philosophy as that which she spoke. I was becoming unnerved, her request frightened me and her assuredness caused me to stutter. I am a man and though women's words have always held sway upon my heart, never like this, not like in this moment. Appalachia spoke again.

"If you are unwilling, if you remain attached to your clothing then do not join me, do not enter the river. Stay on the banks where I shall leave you so I may dilute myself into that Ocean."

"No, Appalachia, you cannot do that. Promise you'll stay with me. Promise you'll not leave me." At the utterance of her next words a piece of me broke inside and even though I was falling apart right before her eyes, dry were the tears

I cried. What follows next are the words that were carried from her lips to rest upon my lobes.

"I promise you I'll always be me." At that moment, on that day, our world came to an end. This became my most desperate hour. I'd never been warned of this; I never knew the path of lovers could be so cruel.

Appalachia then approached me, understanding the gravity of her words, understanding the magnitude of her actions, she approached. She took both of my hands and came forward to my lips, a salutary kiss before departing. I'll never forget the scent of her on our final embrace. Then she spoke to me.

"We do not own one another so let us not play the part. We have simply been blessed with each other's presence until this day came. Besides, if you truly knew, you would understand that we reside within each other and we can never be separated nor have we ever met for a first time. We'll always be so do not get caught up in the time we've spent because our Love we cannot exhaust."

Even though I watched her swim away that day, I still believe she is with me. To this very moment I still hold her close inside. I keep telling myself that maybe one day I'll find the courage to discard the clothing of this world and follow my heart. But until that day comes, I am still thinking of you, I still dream of my Appalachia.

Feelings

and I cannot describe this feeling inside -
like a feather brushing softly against my
lungs, every breath I take shudders
with the love I have for you - but frustrating it is
because I can never adequately express
how it feels or what it is or how it moves -
because even though I touch you,
it is not in the way I would like - and even though
I love you, some promises never see the light -
and I know we try as we retire within each other -
into your temple I enter, closing the doors on the
world, to engage in the act of sensual worship

and so it is, the interlocking of hips, a precursor to,
the unlocking of gifts, we reserve for few -
and once the spirit has been liberated
and our love expressed as we lie together,
contemplating the manifestation of desire
in two people, I feel off - I feel I have cheated you - because
even though your eyes twinkle with the glow
of blessed satisfaction, I still have yet to give you
a taste of this feeling I have, this feeling inside
that is so difficult to describe - this feeling that
is uniquely reflected in our honest embrace

sweet disappointment it is because it means my prayers
have not been answered and we must worship together
again - sweet disappointment it is as I kiss you upon your
neck to arouse your expectations of what is to come next -
my love, make sure the doors are locked tight
because I feel I can praise you all night

Love's Martyr

My love, I have forgotten you a thousand times but yet, I still speak of you. And when I speak of you, I speak of us because in the process of forgetting you I have forgotten myself. Though I feel it is our destiny to be apart; I cannot help but fight to be with you. You have become my final horizon on this perpetual eleventh hour of the heart. Why must it be this way? Why is love a double-edged sword?

There was a time our love brought us close, it made us one, I cared for you. I never felt as necessary as in the moments I held you within my arms. Snuggled against me, in the chill of an autumn night, I became your most sought after comforter. How beautiful we were; how beautiful you are. Though vast my imagination, I could not conceive of a life without you; my heart could not fathom an existence in exile—in exile from you. But alas, the blade of love was twisted and our intentions became askew.

There was a time you embraced my touch but now, you recoil from my stare. There was a time my words were a melody unto your ears but now, you've retreated to a distance my voice cannot follow. Why does love do this? Why does love cause those so close to remain so far? Or is it that those so far remain so close?

This pain, this love, synonymous and yet, antonymous. Because one edge causes a pain I suffer in your absence but yet, the other edge causes a pain I endure in your presence. Synonymous because of the torture the dual edges both render unto my heart; antonymous because of the polarity that resides within the twist. I would love to be with you but I cannot, the blade has been twisted.

I can think of a thousand reasons not to continue loving you and only one reason to love you. But I find that one is enough because here I am still thinking of you; here I am, still in love with you. And yes, my love for you is real but so is the pain. I think of intoxicating myself but it is hopeless, I am already intoxicated by you.

Our love is a stray bullet, it harms those we never intended to hurt and it maims those who do not deserve such tragedy. And I know you did not mean this, I know you did not wish me to endure such sorrow nor I did you. But do not worry, I am strong; do not worry, I'll suffer alone. I promise you it is not as bad as I make it out to be—it is much worse. But damn it, I will not sit here to become love's martyr.

A Night's Quest

I'm in search of Love. I once knew her but she abandoned me for reasons unknown. But our break was not clean nor was it final, for I see traces of her all around. I see the jovial fluttering of hearts alleviating the ground of lovers' steps. I see nostrils opened wide like nets cast into the sea, praying to catch the scent of the one lovers long for. And I see eyes, bright as the sun, shedding light on the shadowed sentiments lovers feel for another. Oh, I see her very well. Love has left her blessings everywhere, except with me.

Though the evidence of her presence rest all about me, I know not where to begin to search for Love. I had been told that if it is Love I seek, the reflection of her identity could be found in the body of a woman so into their bodies I searched. With great pleasure and enthusiasm I discovered and rediscovered the body of a woman. Their topography I became familiar with, charting their responses, their movements, what made them tense and what brought them ease, I took note of it all. A modern day conquistador was I.

Though the volumes of my conquest grew in depth and the expanse of my territory swelled in size, within the body of a woman, Love I could not find. Though continuously I fell deep within them, the mystery and magic of falling became lost on me. Accustomed I had become to the hills I climbed and the valleys I delved. One began to look like another and soon I understood that there was nothing more to be discovered, I had seen it all. Though possessing a body covered in the scars of my romantic endeavors, Love could not or would not, find a wound to enter.

Love, she no longer enchants me, I am too familiar with her ways. Where has the novelty gone? Where is her beauty?

It is all routine now, no poetry, no excitement, no more revelations of worlds unknown. Love was once a voyage of exploration and discovery but now, she has become a campaign of conquest and seduction.

Tonight I seek a queen or possibly a lost maiden needing a home for the night. My search for Love has been relegated to this because it is a simple task for men to constitute themselves to the next best thing if they fail in their original endeavors. If not Love then it is nothing, for the heart shall make way for obsession, lust and all the carnal desires. But do not blame us, for we are blameless. We seek only simplicity and in lust, we are offered just that.

For lust can be more honest than love. Love often does not understand itself, it does not understand its reasons and remains unsure of its own intentions. Often love is fickle and known to be unreliable. Love has the tendency to lie to itself and thus, causing love to lie to others. Love simply knows how to love but knows nothing of Love. But with the carnal desires but with lust, you can always be assured of their intentions and you can always be assured of when they shall end.

So here I am, on a night's quest, in search of Love or the next best thing. They say that the eyes are the windows to the soul and this is especially true for women and romance. So I quickly become a peeping tom, glancing into women's eyes, hoping to catch their desires laid bare before me. For some, deciphering a female's visual code is easy. But for me it is a challenge surpassed only by my quest for Love. Oh no, I can read the visual signs women want me to catch quite easily but the challenge is in deciphering the motivations behind these optical illusions.

For what reasons do her eyes beckon me? Is it her self-esteem that needs a boost or does she plan on making me her personal bank teller for the night? Maybe she is one who enjoys attracting suitors for no other purpose than to serve her own vanity, a monger of attention, that pulls a man's rope all through the night just to snip it clean as she leaves to join her accustomed companion. Or I could possibly be a course meal for her eyes with no intent of purchasing the dessert. For whatever reason she beckons, it is essential to decode her intentions, for twenty minutes spent with a tease is twenty minutes lost to the night.

But I do understand the purpose for these optical illusions. The heart is a fragile gem and in the coarse hands of an egocentric seducer, it can be shattered. So with these illusions you guard your heart until you are sure of my intentions, until you have peered into my soul. But rest assured, I seek not your services for a lonely night. If given the chance, when it comes to love, I can be a master artisan.

Now then, let our hearts dance in the backdrop of these visual effects and criminal intents. For to bear false witness is a crime and we both know our actions attest to a different incentive than the one that rest within our minds. Because behind our play of words and coy demeanor, remains veiled our true intentions on the night. We act now in a manner socially acceptable and personally respectable but there is very little acceptable or respectable about the acts we wish to commit behind closed doors.

But alas, it has not come to that, yet. As I said, it is a challenge, a challenge that escalates in difficulty when coupled with my earnest desire for Love. It is a search that I have not forsaken; it is a task I continue to endure. So on the night I resemble a chimera, some sort of hybrid creature ethereal in mind but primal in nature. As I approach, my intentions are pure but become carnally tainted in proximity to you. I promise I am spiritual in desire but sensual in execution. I'll try not to misbehave, believe me, I'll do my best but you must take my hand to show me the way.

Some give me the charge of being a womanizer but that is inaccurate. Love gave me these eyes for a purpose that I intend to fulfill. With these hands I distinguish what is false from what is real. I see purpose in the curves that appropriate your hips so masterfully. I see the promise of life Love has entrusted upon your bust. So if my eyes fall to distraction from your own, please take no offense at my glances, do not deem me uncouth. For my eyes are only doing what they were created to do and like wise, they offer a silent compliment to the craftsmanship of your own artistry. My interest in you is the sum of this physical equation and for that, I will not apologize.

But maybe there are alternative reasons my eyes fall away from your own. I see your smile, I view your approach but I resist. I know the purpose that lies behind your pupils, I know where you want to take me, I know where you want to go but I cannot, I will not allow it. Though I seek Love, I will not allow myself to become Love's fool, again.

So I, prematurely, turn away from your stare. You take my actions for shyness but no, I am afraid. Of what, you may ask. Of falling, I would reply. I try to convince myself that this cowardly act is justified; there is good reason I retreat from the very aim for which I am here. It is far more often that the prospect of what could be is more attractive than that which actually becomes. So I will not waste my time with you; this is what I tell myself. But I cannot help but think there are also times when something beautiful can come from nothing.

And so the pursuer has become the pursued; you will not cease. You discard my resistance and break through my fear. You try to catch a glimpse of the soul behind the eyes but I rarely make direct contact, I do not allow you to get that close. Nothing good ever comes from allowing another into your world, the precious world we have reserved for ourselves. Not that close, there is no room for you here though there is a vacancy.

I apologize, dear maiden, for I know not what I want, I know not what I desire. And for this reason, complications arise within my heart and now they involve you. Do not become tangled in my world, do not allow yourself to become lost in me, I beg you. Save yourself the trouble, for I am a troubled soul in search of the very thing I fear most, Love. She has crippled me before and she is the only one that has the power to cripple me again.

So please, save yourself, please save me the trouble of rejecting your advances before we both become involved in something we do not mean. Do not mean? Yes, do not mean, for it only takes a moment for me to know if you are the type soul I could fall for and it pains me to say but the verdict is no. I am a drifter, a ghost of a lover because I am unable to manifest myself in that which I desire-Love.

And you sense it too, a lacking in my soul. A lacking you have not felt before. Where is my heart, you ask. It was taken, shattered and then dispersed by that enchantress, Love. I know it was punishment but for what, I do not know. So though I may be capable of loving you proper, I cannot love you in full. For I have not the heart to reciprocate your love nor can you provide me with the inspiration to pursue a love that touches the soul and does not merely drunken the heart.

Oh what a curse I bear, possessing the inability to fall and get lost in Love. And it seems so easy for others, why is it so difficult for me? I see souls falling in love all around but I had the misfortune of not being born so clumsy. What is the use of a soul without a heart to love? What is the use of a soul without a heart to know thyself?

Regardless of my warnings and against my protest, you confide in me. You confide in me, despite everything I've said, for I have confused a queen for a maiden. You tell me that you think you no longer believe in Love. My sentiments you can relate to because they reflect your own. I am befuddled, words line my tongue but I know not what to say. But you speak volumes as you take my hand and lead me home.

And now we are alone to continue the conversation we left abridged on a night's quest. I speak words of hope, I speak faith to you, I tell you Love is real, I know it. I tell you that I once knew Love but in time, I have forgotten her. I look into the eyes of this queen, I look to the soul I had mistaken for a maiden. In your eyes I see begging, they are begging to believe me, begging to be with me, begging to release me. I speak to you.

I tell you that I love you, when we both know it is not true. But you accept it, you accept it to become a part of your dream, a part of your hopes. You want to believe; you want to believe in Love. You want to believe so desperately that you allow me to lie to you as I lie with you. We both say words we do not mean but within our lies, I feel truth. The truth is in our desire, our desire to believe. We lie about Love, not that we no longer believe in Love but it seems Love no longer believes in us. So we decide that even though we are not in love we can fake it for the night. It'll be our honest lie.

And so it is, I become your lovers' isle. I am the place to which you retreat to forget your pains and frustrations with Love. I am your safe haven; you feel secure in my arms. You, who met me from afar, came to me, believing that I could provide you with comfort, believing I could express to you, love, in a way that is rarely displayed in your life. You love me for this, you love me for my patience, you love me for my company, you love me for the lips but more so, the ear I lend you.

I am a perceptive lover and that is the initial step to becoming an excellent lover. I seek to understand your soul's condition. I need to know your ailments so that I may become your cure. In inaudible ways your heart speaks to me; it describes your symptoms. And I listen; I listen attentively. Because that's what women desire most, a man who will listen, earnestly, to the thoughts of their heart. And once you have rested, recovered and had your fill of me, you'll go back, back to the world from which you came.

How unfortunate it is that all the love that draws you near is the same love that tortures me daily. For I am your lovers' isle and never your lover. But it is cool, everything will be all right because I promise to stay committed to you until I no longer am. And the day will come when you'll decide to leave because you'll finally realize that you cannot open the heart of a soul that no longer possesses one. I cannot be the in depth lover you wished me to be. I cannot be the authentic soul you desire and so you'll leave.

And this will be the day, this will be the exact moment I'll scream to you as you walk away, "Wait! I am that guy, I am the one you need me to be, I am the lover you've been searching for. I just don't know where he is; I just don't know where I am. What I'm trying to say is I just don't know-where is Love." Then you'll turn to me to say...

"Quest on, my friend, quest on."

Blind

Though I cannot see you, I cannot deny the love I feel for you. It is like a calling, a soft whisper to the heart that comes from a place unknown. This is why I say I love you though I do not know you. How can you love someone that you do not know? Well I do know this feeling inside is a reflection of you; it is a piece of your energy that you've given me. What did I do to deserve such a blessing? What did I do to deserve such a fate?

I asked questions about you that no one could answer. I sought for you, I asked others where you could be found but every place they sent me, you were no longer there. Where have you gone? Are you true? I want to know because I love you and yet, I barely know you.

Is this a lie? Am I merely infatuated with this fire inside, this fire that has been burning within me since my youth, since before the earliest memories of myself? Am I alone in this burning? Am I the only one that feels you in such a way, that is pulled to you in such a way, that loves you in such a way?

They worship you but not like I do. They praise you but not like I do. They call upon your name but not like I do. Before I can speak a syllable, your presence rushes upon me like the sight of my beloved in youth.

In secret, you slip into my soul and rest with me throughout the days and nights. You hold me close and comfort me in a manner that only you can. Your kisses soothe me even when I feel alone. And yet, I do not know you. You are the greatest of blessings and my closest friend. I pray that I am forever drawn to you until I no longer am.

But In This Room...

There was a time a piece of him would slip away whenever he saw her. There were days a part of him would die whenever he thought of her. And when he looked into her eyes, she was gone, possibly never to return again. But in this room they are together and the storied history of their desolate affair shall have no claim over the pages that shall be written on this night.

They do not mind if their love is like forbidden poetry and their passion, the very blasphemous utterances that reverberate through the heavens above. To Love they request, "If our actions are premature then chastize us tomorrow, for we shall sin tonight." But Love condemns them not, for they are lovers and it is for this purpose they have been created.

Possessing such sacred beauty, he feels to touch her would be profane but she takes him by the hand, easing all concerns and guides him upon her. He becomes enveloped by her love as she melts upon the fire that is him. He is like the roots of a tree, digging deep for the essence of life, nestled between the corridors of love. They flow together like waves against the sand, breaking through the threshold of love's shore, washing away all thoughts of the world outside.

The earth has lost hold of their bodies as it trembles beneath their feet. The solitude of the sky is shattered by love cries from the heart. But this is not a case of hearing much thunder and witnessing no rain; this she truly enjoys as she soaks in all that he is. And through this torrent of passion, through this storm of ecstasy, her body remains softer than the clouds of the sky.

He whispers her name in an act of disbelief. For so long

he's searched for this moment; for so long he's sought the mysteries of this room. And now he has her; now they have each other. She has taken the form of many women before, so many women and he has dreamt of them all. Confusing their image with her but that is the way of Love.

Love motivated him she drove him to reach beyond who he was to become who he is. Love taught him not to become attached to one of her myriad of forms because once he had possessed that image, she would be gone. Love moved on and so would he.

He chased her; he chased her many forms and each time he'd possessed her, she would change. Love never remained constant; she was never the same. Love always altered her essence once he had taken hold of what he had sought to possess but this was no fault of Love. Her consistency or lack thereof, was the deception of his own heart. As he grew in maturity as he grew in understanding, he came to realize that Love was always true and it was he that had not remained constant.

He became so focused on his pursuit of Love that he did not realize the change occurring within his own soul. That is the nature of Love; that is her true beauty. She took him to places he never knew existed within himself, for the truest love drove so deep into him that in her pursuit he stripped away the exterior of himself to reveal the most of himself. He gave up the whole of himself to discover the mystery of himself because it took all of his self to realize such a purpose, to realize such a destiny as Love.

She is the deepest secret, the most sacred treasure, the authentic meaning of life. And no soul is allowed to touch such a purpose except those that are true to themselves, the ones who are true to Love. Love brought about the improvement of his soul and he ended up discovering he was so much

Echoes of a Whisper

more than he had ever conceived or experienced. That is the mark of true love and in this room he had her—formless, beautiful and infinite, he had her and she had him. They were not in love; they were Love.

"Finally," as tears stream from her eyes, he wonders what he has done wrong, never possibly considering that he has committed the ultimate right. At a loss of breath she exhales the words, "thank you." He knows not what she means but at least he knows this is right. "Thank you," an expression of gratitude for him because he has released her, he has released her from her prison, her prison of love.

Those are not tears of sorrow she cries; they are not tears of pleasure or of pain. Those are the tears of a free lover reflecting the pure, sweet taste of liberation to a soul that has starved a life time for a love such as this. She has not the breath to express the words she wishes to say so her tears write the inscription along the side of her cheeks. She needed him, she needed a man that would search her through, not to exploit her treasure but to unveil her Truth.

Her heart stirs for him; it is inspired by him. Through his lips she can taste his soul; in his eyes she witnesses eternity. In the world she feeds the mouth of a thousand souls but in this room it is he that satisfies her every appetite, it is Love that is all she needs. But she is an experienced lover and understands the ways of love. She knows how eternity can slip away in the course of a night. But for now, they lie in silence, cherishing the moment, having forsaken time.

No words are spoken between them, no "I love you's," no "you're so beautiful's." Tonight, in this room, only the truth is spoken. Because lovers say so much more than lips could ever utter and this moment shall not be hindered by words. For in this moment they are all that exist and all that needs be. Outside of this room there is nothing but in this room are all things eternal. For this is a moment held everlasting in the hearts of all lovers.

It is the first time you make love...and actually mean it.

The Rundown

You are who you are for a reason, now find it.

It all started on February 1st 1997. You're a fourteen-year-old freshman at North Gwinnett High School sitting in Dacula High School's old gym watching the varsity basketball team play. You're resting from the JV game you just played and you're now looking for things to get into, like always, while the varsity team plays their game.

Right now your attention is on a girl you use to be involved with who is a water girl on the varsity boys' team. She's looking back at you during the game and your interest has hit its peak. Even though y'all are not together anymore, right about now you're seriously considering rectifying that situation. You may be a Christian but you're also a man and this is one of those times the flesh is starting to get the better of you.

While you're sitting in the stands, contemplating love's conquest, you notice one of your friends listening to a cd. You take a look at the case and notice it is a group you've heard about. Outkast is the name of the group and ATLiens is the album. You've heard a couple of their singles and you especially like the single that holds the same name as the album title. After your friend has finished listening to the cd you ask him if you could check it out, to see if the rest of the album is as good as the singles.

Your friend allows you to listen to the album without hesitation and you pop the cd in and press play. You're instantly caught up in the intro to the album, which is original and unlike any production you've heard before. This duo from Atlanta, Georgia has a distinct style and sound of music that is innovative and in a sense, deep and aesthetically pleasing.

Over the course of the next hour you listen to the entire cd without skipping a track because with every track something is there to keep your attention and you just have to keep listening. The girl who had your attention, earlier in the evening, looks back at you a couple of times but you are gone. I mean you are there but your mind is caught up in the music.

You can relate to these guys. You feel what they are saying and they reflect a spirit that you feel lives within yourself. They're artists who say things you would like to recite over a track and they teach things you believe should be heard. Without hesitation, the next chance you get, you hit the music store and buy the Outkast ATLiens cd. It is an hour's worth of easy-going, southern style, thought-provoking jams and verses.

Now that you have the cd you take a look at the cd cover and flip through the booklet that has all the credits to each song. Before the song credits you find a comic book style story portraying Outkast as a couple of prophesied intergalactic heroes. You read through the comic and you're astonished, you've never seen anything as creative as this in an album booklet. Now you are even more enamored with the innovative spirit of the artists.

A couple of months go by and obviously, you are still listening to ATLiens every chance you get. Outkast have become the flagship artists for your particular taste in music, especially hip-hop but you begin to notice something. You still enjoy listening to the album straight through but recently you have been getting visions. Well, not so much visions but rather a story. A story has been developing in your head with each subsequent listen to the ATLiens cd. The story sort of mimics the comic from the cd booklet but even stranger, it is directed by each track you listen to. Each track contributes a different setting and scene for the story but they all run together in a coherent way. Before you know it you have an entire story, inspired by the ATLiens album, running through your mind.

The story is like an extended music video that runs throughout the course of the album. In your mind, characters are created and events unfold as they blend in with the spirit of the music. Now you go back to the ATLiens cd as often as possible to listen to the whole thing so that more of the story can be replayed and revealed to you through the music. You do not yet realize it but this story is about to change your life forever.

Dream Deepened

You've always been a writer; you began writing heartfelt poems at the age of twelve. On the surface you were a goof ball, everyone knew you for saying and doing stupid stuff just to get a laugh. But underneath it all, was something deep. You, and others, didn't discover it until that first poem you wrote. You enjoyed the attention you garnered because of your writing. The poem wasn't that impressive but for a twelve-year-old, it was a bit against the norm.

You kept writing whenever you felt the spirit and you eventually began writing rhymes. They were a bit more of a challenge but that just made it all the more enjoyable when you wrote one that you could hang your hat upon. This same spirit, which motivated you to write from the heart, felt akin to the spirit inspiring the story rapidly developing in your head.

A year has gone by since your introduction to ATLiens. You've written your first heartfelt rhyme and moved into the basement as a sixteenth birthday present from your folks. Concerning the story, not much has changed. You still listen to the cd just to replay the story in your mind as a point of relaxation and reflection.

Then, one day you hear that a group called Goodie Mob is about to drop their second album. You know of Goodie Mob because they are featured on a couple of the songs for the ATLiens cd. You find out later that they are a part of a larger contingent of artists known as the Dungeon Family which consists of various Atlanta-based artists including Outkast, Goodie Mob, Organized Noize and various other creators from Atlanta.

You figure that if Goodie Mob is in leagues with Outkast they may have something to offer you in a spiritual sense through their music. You've heard their first two singles "Black Ice" and "They Don't Dance No Mo" and you don't think twice about buying the album Still Standing. The album is nice, never providing a moment of regret for purchasing the cd but this is the point where things start to grow thick.

You're not sure if it's a coincidence or you are just mentally somehow doing this on purpose but another story begins to develop in your head, this time based and influenced by the Goodie Mob Still Standing album. At first you're like, "Wow, this is interesting. Well, at least I now have a sequel to the original," but it doesn't stop there.

The following summer, after your sophomore year at North Gwinnett, you and the boys' basketball team are taking your annual trip up to Middle Tennessee State University for a basketball camp. It's a decently long ride, especially in a large van so listening to music is a norm to pass the time.

You notice that one of your teammates has the first Goodie Mob album, Soul Food and he allows you to check it out. Almost in the exact same method the ATLiens album took you away, the Soul Food album is an experience for you in and of itself. So it doesn't come as a surprise to you that yet another story begins to develop in your mind. Of course this story is based on Soul Food.

Now you know that these stories are not a coincidence. You don't know whether it is because you are just being inspired and creating the stories yourself or that there is something purposeful and unique in your listening to these albums. But what you do know is that something special is going on in your life and you want to know why. Are these stories a gift from a source beyond your comprehension or a product of an actively creative mind? In either case, you know that you enjoy the stories and you have made a conscious decision to one day get them out of your mind and down on paper but that summer has more in store for you.

Later that summer, your heart begins to become disturbed and uneasy. It begins to speak to you but not like an audible voice but rather through feelings, deep emotional feelings. The feelings are real and they become extremely clear and direct to you. It has to be God or so you begin to believe.

Nominally you are a Christian but the lust you possess inside does not reflect this sentiment. And your mind is rarely occupied with thoughts of appeasing God. You go through the motions of being a Christian; church on Sunday, Bible study on Wednesday, revival in May, Vacation Bible School in June and Christmas Cantata in December. You're basically just being an active participant in your church but recently, it hasn't gone much deeper than that. When you were younger, you were very attentive to God and enjoyed reading the Bible but as you got older, a few things changed.

But now you have this feeling inside and you attribute it to God. Even though you're a Christian, you have never been sure in the reality of a supernatural being that prevailed over all of existence. Your belief in God was more hopeful than assured. You possess a heart that is truly not that evil or deviant; it's just that you are still unsure about God. Though you pray often, who are you speaking to? Is it God or are you just talking to yourself?

Never mind your previous disposition, whether God or not, you are sure that your heart is speaking to you right now. The message is clear and brings fear to you. Recently you have discovered the hatred that still lies deep at the core of humanity, a hatred that drives people to detest and kill those unlike them. And now, your heart is telling you that one day you must face this hatred and become a mediator. And, without doubt you know you may very well be hated for what you do and you know you may very well be killed for what you do but your heart says that following the will of God is vastly more important than thoughts of self preservation. You argue with your heart, you ask it to give this task to another and just let you be. But who are you but a servant?

Through your heart more is revealed to you; you know you are not ready to do what you must do, you must patiently wait until the time comes for you and this time will come quite a few years down the road. With no reason, the ages twenty-six and twenty-seven become significant to you and you keep this in your heart. You ask if the story will play a significant role in this plan or is it something of your own creative device? The answer is honest and clear; the story is meant for you but the spirit within you is meant for the world. Then you feel the emotional voice leave from within until the time approaches for you to do whatever it is you are going to do.

Complications

Your junior year begins with much anticipation because Outkast's third album is getting ready to drop. You never came to imagine that ATLiens was not Outkast's first album but instead you find that Southernplayalisticadillac-muzik was Outkast's debut album. Without thought you go out and buy the first Outkast album a few weeks before the third one is released and on both occasions the story is continued in your mind. Finally things develop deeper, the story goes in order of the releases. Southernplayalisticadillacmuzik, Soul Food, ATLiens, Still Standing and now, Aquemini make up five different books within the story. And without provocation you know that there will be seven in all, most likely the next Goodie Mob album, and then something different. You feel the last album will not be an Outkast album but something else. Your hope is that maybe the Dungeon Family will get together and do a compilation album. You believe that a compilation album is where all this will eventually lead. Another thing becomes apparent to you now; the story has taken on a more personal meaning. The main character in the story, to which most of the events occur, is now understandably a reflection of you. The story itself is the portrayal of your life through the fantastical images created in your mind. This understanding brings you to the brink of anticipation and though you planned on putting off writing the story until you were older, you can no longer wait. In the fall semester of your junior year in high school, you begin writing the story.

The process is not smooth and even though you had already written down pages of notes concerning the story, it still does not flow out the way you anticipated it would. Your efforts begin with the part of the story inspired by Southernplayalisticadillacmuzik. You now introduce characters and ideas into the story that existed in your mind before you first listened to ATLiens. The first draft is written in script form and even though the task is difficult, you do enjoy working on the story.

Your junior year brings about other complications to your life in the form of love. Two different loves but the one noted here will be that of the basketball program. So much of your life and time is given to the basketball team, it's very demanding. The game is so demanding that your heart is eventually forced to choose between this feeling you have inside and basketball. After much painful deliberation, you choose your faith. Your heart remains with the feeling but you are encouraged by your teammates and coaches to stay on the team and you do—a decision that you would not regret. But you now know that which is the top priority in your life, the feeling inside.

As you continue writing the story, it quickly becomes apparent that a strictly literary format will not be able to convey the spirit behind the ideas in your head. Written words cannot capture the sound, motion and feel of the story. It will take a different medium to convey this world inside your mind. You would need a medium able to present the content of the story in a visually engaging way, along with providing sound to which the story was primarily based on, music. The story was being played inside your mind like an extended music video but the content of the story ran deeper than that which could be expressed in a video. It would take a movie.

A movie—that was the only way possible to convey this story. This movie could not be observed by the audience like a passive spectacle; the story was not for entertainment. This movie would have to be more than just a show; it would have to be participatory. The audience would have to become part of the movie. You have an idea how to do this but it is not yet time to approach that thought. So after your first failed attempt at translating the story from the psychological realm of your mind to the physical realm of the world you turn your attention to other interest in life.

Slipping Away

It has now been well over a year since you felt the presence speak to you in reference to what you would have to do in the future. Your first failed attempt at conveying the story left you open to other interest—girls, basketball—but beyond all of that you had an aim in religion. You feel that you should be doing something to prepare yourself for the future mission, even though your heart asked you to be patient and informed you that you were not ready. But also contained within your heart is this unsatiated desire.

You are a Christian; this is your announced faith. But Christianity is not the only religion that exists in the world. There are others, numerous others but you wonder, which faith is true. Obviously being a Christian, your answer is clear. Christianity is the truth but then, why so many other faiths? Obviously there must be numerous flaws in them leaving Christianity as the true faith that stands alone. And there it is—you have something to occupy your time until it is time to do what you are supposed to do. You will research and study the various other religions and identify their flaws so you can prove Christianity is the one true faith.

So you purchase a book on the world's religions and its focus is on the major religions of the world; Daoism, Buddhism, Hinduism, Islam, Judaism, and Confucianism (which in truth is not a religion but rather a code of ethics). You read through the book and take notes on the other religions. You become interested and enthralled with all of these different ideas you are finding. The one thing you are truly not finding is faults.

Yes, there are differences in the various beliefs concerning the faiths but when it comes down to morals and ethics, there is hardly a significant case to be brought against them. In more than a few ways, their teachings are almost identical, in nature, to Christianity. But simply because they seem like Christianity does not make them Christianity. There are definite differences and only one faith can hold true.

Christianity teaches that Jesus is the truth and the life and no one will be accepted by the Father (the one true God) except through His son (Jesus). If Christianity is the only way to God then why are the other faiths so morally upright in their beliefs and teachings? Why would God allow for such faiths to have developed and become rivals to God's spoken word in the Bible? And if God is omnipotent then why is the only avenue to Him through Jesus? Why is God restricted in such a manner? Can there be no other way? Is it even possible for an omnipotent God to be limited in His ability to provide multiple paths to Him? Why would God then exclude all faiths, except Christianity, when it comes to the path of attaining Him?

You play the scenario back through your mind and realize that you may very well be lucky for having been born into a Christian family and into a country predominantly Christian in faith. You think to yourself, what if I had been born in India? As difficult as it is for many people's beliefs to be swayed by a foreign faith, would God condemn me on the simple fact that I was born a Hindu or Buddhist and truly believed my faith was right beyond all others? How many Christians take this exact same stance and approach to the ideals of foreign beliefs in comparison to their own?

The God you knew was not like this. You knew God and you knew God's love was boundless. God's love was far too deep for the teachings of a doctrine to limit its expansion to all souls. To now believe that God's love and acceptance would only be limited to one particular faith, in the very exclusion of others which are righteous in their own path, is unacceptable for you.

If this is truth and God cannot be reached except through Christianity in this manner, then you decide that you cannot and will not serve a God that is discriminate with His love and mercy in this way. You decide you would rather die and go to hell than serve a God that became so exclusive with the gift of love.

You know there is good in many souls that are not Christians, and you refuse to serve a God that punishes the faith in all of these people. Your heart will not accept a God like that. If this is the proper interpretation of the Bible then you know what you must do, you understand the conviction of your heart. You renounce the faith of your youth and the spirit you once possessed. You're a Christian no more.

The Mask

You are eighteen, having just graduated high school, preparing for college and you have just recently renounced your faith. What is there left to do? Your heart is terribly disturbed because of your lost faith. In the coming years, you will cry more over the absence of your belief in God than any other issue in life. This cannot be how it ends; this is not acceptable. You must begin a quest; you must search for God. You must find God because there in lies your deepest love in life.

You decide to major in religion at Georgia State University so you may be instructed, and challenged, in faith. You are determined to find an answer to whatever it is you are looking for and you already know your soul will suffer horribly because of this determination. You're dying inside and you can feel it.

The absence of God's love is beginning to take a toll on your heart and spirit. You do not wish to disturb any of your close friends with your ill disposition so you decide to mask the true feelings inside. The pain is deep but you don't want to bring anyone else's spirit down because of what you now lack in your life. You don't know the truth so it is best you allow those who believe to be kept safe in their belief, the weight of their spirit will remain light for it. But as for you, the suffering will come and it will be deep.

So your freshman's year in college begins without much change. You go through the motions of school while working on the story whenever you are inspired. But you're still bothered by the absence and this leads you to a thought. Maybe the story is what led you away from God. Maybe you are more dedicated to the story than finding God. This could all just be in your head but you can't tell what's real and what's not, anymore. The only way to make sure that the story is not the problem is to throw all of it away. And that's exactly what you do. You throw everything, you have ever written, away. You throw away the poetry you wrote when you were young, the rhymes, the notes on the story and all writing that you composed concerning the story. Everything you had ever written from your heart, for the past six years, was now gone. Everything that meant the most to you, in essence was you, is now gone.

You feel a bit better after your episode of catharsis and your heart feels honest. It was painful to let go of all that work which meant so much to you but you feel better about your search for God and you need to know if it was the story that drove God away.

Two months pass and your life is running its course. You feel no closer to finding whatever it is that you are looking for but you do notice something, it's coming back. The story, the desire to write the story is coming back. It returns not of your own will but it feels right, it feels necessary. It feels like this is what you are supposed to do, write the story. And this is what you do, two months after throwing everything away, you begin to write the story again. This time you write with the certainty that you are meant to compose this story, you are supposed to bring the story to life. No more abortion, one day this story will come to life in one form or another.

True Love

Your freshman year ends and you move on through the summer toward your sophomore year. You have begun work on an official second draft to the story, while also falling in love again. This time is deeper than the first and it is with someone who will always mean something to you. But you still have problems, you still are not satisfied. You try to ignore the feeling but even in love, you still do not feel complete.

You begin talking to friends about the situation because it is beginning to get in the way of simply living and enjoying your life. You tell one person that you need something to fight for, love alone is not enough. But you don't have anything to fight for, you don't possess that spirit of the past. It's probably gone forever.

One friend advises you to get drunk once and see if that doesn't change some things. You've never been drunk before and it was an experience you really didn't care much for having anytime soon. Besides, even though you've never had the experience, you already know that this problem is too deep for drinking to solve.

In other news, you finally have all seven of the albums, that will contribute to the story, in your possession. The sixth album is Goodie Mob's World Party, which coincidentally goes perfectly with the ideas you personally were having for the sixth installment to the story. The ideas you were having were a global concept in which the world became somehow involved and the Goodie Mob album agreed with your ideas as if tailored. The seventh album also agreed with the ideas you were having about the seventh piece to the story. You listened to Outkast's fourth album, Stankonia and as you expected, a consistent story did not play through your mind when listening to the cd, though the album was nice.

So a little over a year passes between the Stankonia release and the final album in the story, which is for you, the much anticipated Dungeon Family compilation album Even in Darkness. You listened to the entirety of the album, and even more so than World Party, the seventh album was fitted for the ideas that you already possessed in your mind. You finally now have the seven albums and the story continues to evolve as you work on it in reality and in your mind.

You have a moment of insight while talking with your mom and you tell her that this story in your head means more to you than anything else in the world, even more than your own parents whom you love dearly. And you also say that whatever this thing is that you're battling, this doubt, this dark emptiness, if you could somehow overcome it you would be a far better soul for having faced it. You cannot lie to yourself and believe in God just for the sake of believing and making yourself feel better. You're not looking for a belief; you're searching for truth. The presence is dark and hidden within you but there is no other choice that you should make in this situation. You must face up to your own fear, pain and doubt, you must face up to yourself.

A few months after all of these conversations you have your first experience of being intoxicated and a little more than under the influence. With your first go 'round on the light-headed side of life you end up tackling a palm tree, getting in a fight with a drink machine and surprisingly you do not have a hangover the next morning—but that's because you're still drunk. The hangover hits you later that afternoon and it hits hard. You make your first promise never to drink again, a promise that you will make several times in the future on the wake of similar nights. But as you figured, this really didn't solve any of the deeper problems vexing your mind and a month from now you will end up having the worst day of your life.

In short, you lose your love in a time when you are having an identity crisis, the identity crisis, the one that you will not end up solving until four years later. In the meantime, you change majors because studying religion is getting you nowhere and it especially lost its appeal after coming out of a classroom where the whole discussion was over what is the difference between a religion and a cult—question, What Does It Matter!?! Besides, religion didn't seem to capture all the aspects of life, it did not deal with all the aspects of the human experience.

You end up picking psychology as your new major because a few friends believed that you would be a decent counselor. You're known as a good listener amongst many of your friends and besides, psychology is a subject that engages and discusses more aspects of the human experience than any other major that you know. But changing majors is not enough for you, you need a change of scenery. You love the ATL and you love G-State. Both the city and the school are places of great potential but you need to break out of your accustomed environment. Basically you want to run away from yourself, instead you do the next best thing. You transfer to the University of Georgia going into your fourth year of college.

Hit & Miss

Upon your first semester at UGA, three things haven't changed: you are still a State Boi at heart, Panther Pride; you've increased your work on the story, even going so far as buying mythology and symbolism books to help you write a back drop to the story in order to fill in the gaps you cannot cover in the main story; and you still feel the pain of absence as always. You can't runaway from yourself so you end up using girls to try and fill the void.

But you notice something, a subject matter that used to be simple for you to solve, ahem, girls have become a highly difficult code to decipher. You don't know why but for some reason your whole approach, courtship and signature is off. Meeting and talking to girls is not as easy as it use to be. And this leads you to making a second mistake, you begin to force things so the whole courtship process seems contrived now. There is nothing natural about your moves, thoughts or words. Everything seems fake and insincere, and it's all because you're set on trying to make something happen when the vibe isn't right. You are so desperate to cover up this emptiness inside, with a relationship, that you continually trip over your own feet and pursue relationships you really don't want to be in.

After a couple of years of this misstep with girls you eventually rediscover your mojo only to discover the reason you didn't have it for so long in the first place. No human in the world could fill the void that the belief in God had left in your heart. And maybe on a subconscious level, you knew this and that's why you felt so insincere and out of step in the past.

In truth, you were chasing after things you really didn't want but your eyes kept you fooled. No matter where your heart lies, it is always difficult to turn away from 36-24-36. Eventually you will understand the mistake you have been making and move on to solve the real problem but even this understanding is still some ways away.

In the meantime, you continue to work on your story and the problem of yourself. You graduate college, get a job out in Memphis and meet a girl while also uncovering more secrets about yourself. In truth, you move out to Memphis to keep things fresh and random so life does not begin to feel too redundant. The story remains top priority in your life and you believe living in a new state may facilitate the search within.

The girl you have met is fun, frank and forward, she lets you know what's on her mind without hesitation. All of which are qualities you've grown to love in women as opposed to girls who enjoy playing emotional games; you know, the type that proves to be more of a headache than worth the time spent—a.k.a. drama prone. But when it comes to you, nothing is simple and this time around will be no different. She notices it too, that another person lives just below the surface of your appearance. During the few conversations you have with her she is intrigued and begins to dig deep below the surface. This is a novel feeling for you, it has been awhile since anyone has been interested in the you that lies just behind the eyes.

During a particularly interesting conversation, she discovers that you are not a Christian and haven't been for the past five years. She doesn't believe you when you say this. Your exterior personality and actions all reflect that of what a Christian should act like but you're not. You begin to tell her snippets of the story you have written here and you tell her that you do not know if the Divine exists or not, you're searching. But you also tell her something else with confidence. In concerning your search you say, "I'm close, I'm real close to finding the answer."

The summer passes and you move back home to Georgia because the job in Memphis just wasn't for you, in more than one way. But what concerns you most is the answer that you know you are so close to finding. While working on the back story which is now called the Book of Existence, you come to a point in your writing in which you need to create a purpose and reason for Existence. All major religions and mythologies have an explanation for why we exist and also reveal the destiny of all things. You have been putting this particular subject off in the Book of Existence because you wanted to come up with something original. You wanted to come up with an explanation for existence no other religion or story has ever come up with.

The moment of inspiration comes to you after reflecting on a song that you listened to earlier in the day. The title of the song is "K.O.S. (Determination)," and it comes from a cd that you bought more than a year prior to this moment. The album is called Black Star by Mos Def and Talib Kweli. You think about the meaning of the title K.O.S. which is an acronym for Knowledge Of Self. Then, almost precariously, the thought stumbles into the doorstep of your mind. "That's it," you think to yourself as you will spend the next few days ironing out the details behind this idea.

In your story, the purpose of Existence will be for the individual components of the Eternal to come to know themselves. Existence is the platform the Eternal uses to discover its self all over again and once this discovery has transpired, all is complete. Perfect, now you have your origin, purpose and destination. Now it's time to move on to that answer you have been searching for in your own life.

Chasing Your Dream

You've moved back in with your parents in the majestic southern state of Georgia. It's funny how African-Americans now take so much pride in a place that holds a history of such oppression, intolerance, societal injustice and prejudices against their kind simply because of their very likeness. But in the same breath, you love being able to meet a group of people you've never known and have them instantly treat you like a close relative they haven't seen in a couple of years. Within thirty minutes you feel like family, they treat you as their own, and the smiles and laughter are not fake, they're genuine. You don't know these people and they don't know you but somehow, you care for them and it's real. Many things have changed in the two hundred plus year history of America and many things have not. But no matter the place, home is home. And guess what, you love home.

So you quickly pick up a job working at Costco because you don't want to rely on someone else to support you, that's simply your male pride kicking in. Besides, you're paying $400 dollars rent just to stay at home with your parents but the thing is, you're thankful for that. They're treating you like an adult and like an adult you have responsibilities. And one of those responsibilities is figuring out what you now want to do with your life. You know, that same problem you couldn't figure out during your five-year stay in college, five years that turned out to be more like an extended stay at a day care center for young adults. And still there is the story.

After returning home, it becomes difficult for you to hide the struggle you've had since graduating high school. It comes out in the form of depression which, at home, your mother can see clearly in your demeanor. At home is where you are at most yourself. Home is the place where you set the mask aside and let the reality show. You do not like being unhappy so you fight like hell for a reason to smile but the weight of the truth lies heavy on your heart.

You think about what if you were able to achieve everything you could possibly want in life, you think about what if you were able to make the story a movie and accomplish all your goals. But every time you think of these things one conclusion is repeatedly met, they do not bring you happiness. Not even the story brings you happiness;

not even love brings you happiness. What will bring back the happiness?

You've lost your taste for life. There is nothing that fulfills your soul. It is all meaningless and vain. Now is the time when you truly understand the spirit of Solomon when he wrote Ecclesiastes. What is the point of anything? Everything that you could possess in this world will one day pass away. Even the memories we hold so dear will be gone once we're gone. Even the human species is finite, whether we live another billion years or just another minute, all things perish, all life is bound by mortality. Who of you, that are reading this question, will be around one hundred years from now to read it again? You think deeply on the subject. Why think of such things? You are only twenty-three years old; you have a lifetime ahead of you. But this is who you are, this is who you always have been.

And now the world is disturbing you, angering you. What's right, what's wrong? Who is to decide what is right and what is wrong? It seems now that people are deciding morality and proper ethics then slapping God's name on the end product. What is right and acceptable in one culture, at one time, may not have been acceptable and proper in another culture at another time. It has always amused you when people complain about others wearing their pants too low or their hats tilted to the side. You think about when it was the norm in Scottish culture for men to wear skirts with no underwear underneath. You wonder how our society would accept that fashion today but of course, we know what is acceptable and what is not.

And now you think on peace; you think on world peace. Something about the concept just doesn't feel right to you; it doesn't feel natural. Think on it, the world is in a constant state of competition and conflict but is somehow balanced in this conflict. Ever since the birth of life, life has been fighting just to stay alive. Your very body is in a constant state of biological warfare but yet, you're still here and you're still functioning—for the most part. Even the plants of the earth compete for the light of the sun. What creature lives without taking a portion of life from another creature? Even vegetarians eat from plants and are plants not alive? It takes life to sustain life. Something must cease to be, in order for something else to continue being.

You think even on the religious philosophies of the world. Even Jesus said he did not come to bring peace but rather, a sword. In the great Hindu piece of literature, the Bhagavad Gita, Krishna instructs Aryuna to do his duty as a warrior and fight because not fighting would be disgraceful and against his dharma, spiritual duty. Mohammad did not hesitate to defend himself and other Muslims when his offenders came to destroy him. Even the land that is recognized for Lao Tzu, the legendary character of Daoism, also gave birth to the legendary book of conflict, The Art of War. And what of the nature of God to the Jews and how He conquered their enemies and punished them for sin? Let's just say you wouldn't want to get on His bad side.

Yes, we are fighters. We are creatures of conflict living in a world of conflict. To deny this fact would be to eagerly embrace a lie. We must fight, it is who we are but let us not forget this question. Whom should we be fighting, each other or our own self?

So now, for the briefest stint, you truly believe that there is no God; there never has been or ever will be. Only the god created in our own imaginations exists. You are now truly a man without God. So what are you to do with your life? You decide to continue working on the story because it is all you have left. No love, no life, no God but at least you have the story. For better or worse, you'll let it sustain you.

But even your non-belief in God doesn't feel right. You have come to accept that this life is just this life and nothing more. You are not scared of ceasing to exist after death but something truly does not feel right even about that concept. You've accepted that life, in general, is meaningless. Life is only what you make and decide, it to be. But none of this makes sense to you. You can't explain it but something just doesn't feel right about that. It has nothing to do with ethics or a need to believe in an after life, it's just something amiss.

Somehow it doesn't make sense; something continues to pull at your heart. There's something about you, there is something about this world that is not set. Yes, all of this could have been at random but why anything at all, but deeper than that, why this unsatiated need to fulfill it all, to explain it all? Coincidence—of course, it could be just that, but something just doesn't feel right about that thought. You don't know why you are doing this but you continue your search. Accepting a life without God is not how this will end for you, that's not the answer to this quest. You don't have to prove God exists, you just have to do what your heart has asked of you and everything else will be.

Providence

So you follow your heart and continue working on the story. Now you have come to a point in which you are ready to begin work on your third comprehensive draft of The Human Experience, the title you have given the story. This will be the most complete draft of the first album, book, to the story you have written. Your ideas have come a long way since you were that naive teenager who believed he would be the greatest writer of his time. You're nowhere close to being that but becoming your true self is more important to you. And for the first time you are also beginning to truly believe in the story, you believe that it can become a reality, it is truly meant for you.

The year 2006 has begun and your work on the first album is in full swing. You plan to have it done by mid March, providing you stay on track and do not become lazy or distracted. You remain on point with the story as March approaches but a spirit of fear creeps into your heart. You still feel incomplete even as you approach the end of the first album. You feel alone and you don't like the feeling at all. You begin to turn to others, again, for comfort but no one is able to help in the way you need help. That responsibility is with you as it has always been your responsibility to solve yourself.

Regardless, you begin to run away from yourself, again. You turn to friends, travel and drinking but nothing helps, especially drinking. You get so drunk one afternoon that you become ashamed of yourself for falling to such a level as to seeking alcohol as a means for solving the problem of your soul. You become as deeply depressed as you were six months prior to this incident. The end is near and you know it. What will you become or will you become?

You have told a friend that you fear the summer of your 24th year because in the story this is a point of death. Something, maybe even you, comes to an end at that time. And you're scared, you're scared of yourself and the darkness within.

You are now close to the completion of the story and begin seeking help getting it published. You admit to yourself that the story is not the greatest piece of literature ever written but, you are satisfied and proud of the work you have done. However, the depression has hit you before the completion of the first album and you have set it aside for the moment. You are not the person you want to be at this point in your life and this bothers you immensely.

You entertain the thought of going to graduate school so that you're not just sitting on a degree but you deliberate further on this thought. School is not right for you, there isn't an educational institution on earth that can teach you what you need to know. There's no need to waste your time, again, being mentally babysat by another university. You understand, all too well, school is not the place to receive the knowledge you seek and to go back would simply be another form of running away from yourself.

You turn back to the first album and complete it this time. You have ditched the prospect of the story becoming a book, you do not believe your writing skills are of par and besides, the publishing avenue is too slim. You consider placing the story in script form but the dice doesn't hit seven on that idea either. However, you refuse to give up and you continue drilling your mind to find a method of bringing this story to life. While in the back of your head, you continue to wonder why you have been given this story in the first place. That is still a mystery you think of from time to time.

It is now summertime and the World Cup has just ended so you no longer have anything to distract you from
yourself. But you're at peace now, you're not stressing as
much over life, mainly because there is no more conflict
over which direction to take it. You shall live and die by the
story. If you cannot make it a reality then you have failed
at life, but you are accustomed to success and failure, and
the thought of failure does not scare you anymore.

You have a moment of disturbance during the summer
and your mother comes to check on you. You converse and
get out some feelings that are on your mind but the conversation leads to other topics of discussion. You're frustrated
at yourself and your continued inability to find whatever it
is that you seek. You believe that you are not the soul you
are supposed to be at this point in your life. Then you have
a moment of insight into your own thoughts when your
mother asks "will what you are looking for finally make
you happy again once you've found it." Your response is
given without hesitation and is straight forward, "I don't
want to be happy. I don't care about being happy; I just
want to find whatever it is that I am looking for." You have
spoken from the heart, happiness doesn't matter to you,
only what is in your heart.

You have begun working on ideas for an internet site
one of your friends advised that you might want to open
for your story. You've kept the thought in your mind for
sometime now, but you are just now beginning to work on
it in earnest. You've recently read the Bhagavad Gita, for
the first time, to highlight particular philosophies which
express the relationship between Hindu thought and your
story. A few days to a couple of weeks after you have read
it, a thought crosses your mind. You begin thinking about
the KOS, which plays a prevalent role in the Book of Exis-

tence and now, The Human Experience. The knowledge of self, you think about the meaning of this phrase and then so effortlessly, almost of due course, a thought crosses your mind. "No way," is your startled response to the thought. "No way," is your secondary response to the thought as it is dumbfounding.

In the coming weeks you go back to the sayings of Jesus in both the canonized Gospels and the gnostic Gospels, you reread the Bhagavad Gita, you look up the Dhammapada which is the sayings of Buddha, you print out the Dao Da Jing which is a prominent Daoist text, you then read Sufi poetry which is a sect within Islam and you follow that by beginning to read the Qur'an itself. And in amazement it all seems so clear now, sitting right there on the pages reflecting the truth that lives within.

It's been said before—in principle, all religions preach generally the same thing. You know, the old tale about the six blind men that took hold of different parts of an elephant. Well now you are seeing the whole elephant for the first time and you can't believe your eyes. It's more than just principle; they are saying the same truth just in their own languages. Their differences are minor because the Truth runs far deeper than that. The soul of the Bhagavad Gita is reflected in the soul of Islam and the soul of Dao is present within the soul of Jesus. They are saying the exact same thing, their differences are inherent in their symbolic translations, a simple reflection of the beliefs and cultures they grew up within. In short, it is the human mind trying to get a grip on those few fundamental truths, which lead to the rediscovery of self. That may be the purpose but the destination is unspeakable, The One True.

You still are held in doubt but the thought amazes you. You find that even in the essays of Ralph Waldo Emerson, the Authentic Soul is reflected and in the Apology of Socrates, the Soul shines. One day, driving home from work, you think on these things that have come to mind. You retrace the thoughts' origin and you find that the story was meant for you. It was the desire to place a purpose of existence, in the story, that differed from all other religions, and mythologies, which led you to this end. It was the KOS and now you have come to find that instead of being different from the ideas of before, it is exactly the same. The story truly has given more to your life than anything else in the world ever could. Many things now become so clear to you so many things.

You understand why the story wouldn't let you go though you had given up on it countless times over. You see why it was meant for you and why it provoked you to believe that it was the most important thing in your life. You understand why you went through those long four years of intense frustration and simply, feeling out of place in the world. You understand why, on so many mornings, you would curse the moment you first woke for the simple fact of having done so. It makes sense now. The story is your vehicle, the story is your duty, the story is you and your efforts for the story have brought you closer to the very thing you were searching for all along. Before, you never really listened to that second verse in the song K.O.S. but you do now.

POV

What is the point of evolution?

I tried but could not find the inspiration to write the following in a poetic fashion. So forgive me but this piece will be spoken with less artistry than the other works. It concerns my thoughts on religion, God, evolution and the ultimate purpose of existence. I've spoken to very few in such a manner as is to follow but through this piece you'll get a glimpse into the world as I see it and the destiny that awaits us all.

You may not believe in evolution but I do because out of all the explanations we have on our origins it makes the most sense to me. So if you doubt please suspend your thoughts for the sake of this discussion and if you do believe in evolution then take the time to ponder this...what is the point?

The simple obvious answer is that evolution is a process which promotes creatures most fit to survive in whatever environment they are born. Being that life, and this world, is in a constant state of change, adaptation is the single greatest trait that promotes survival. This is why humans have become the most dominate species in the world—because of our ability to adapt to a diversity of environments due to our evolved minds. But is survival the sole purpose of evolution?

If survival is the purpose of evolution then why does religion exist? Is religion a mistake, or byproduct, of the evolved human mind? I've read that not a single society, in the history of human culture, has existed for over three generations without developing some sort of belief in a higher being. Any culture that did not develop such a belief did not survive. So what does this mean? Is religion essential to our survival or is it a mistake that happened to develop within every sustained human culture? Well, to consider religion a mistake, or essential to life, would require us to assume that we know the purpose of evolution.

What is the purpose of surviving? What is the purpose of living? Why do we consider the continuation of life a necessity? Does it really matter if we all died tomorrow? What goal does the continuation of life help us to achieve besides the perpetuation of a redundant plot line? What is so important about living and continuing life? What is the point? Why has evolution found it so essential for us to adapt to survive if surviving is our only cause? What advantage does life offer us in comparison to death?

We are alive...ok who cares? Are we any better than an inanimate rock that is kicked along the side of a street? Yes we are alive and have experiences, some good some bad, but what evolutionary advantage does that give us over a rock? Yes we have the ability to manipulate, kick and throw rocks but once again, who cares? I know the rock does not care because it is not a sentient being. It does not mind if it is kicked, thrown or spat upon. So, is there something else we are supposed to do besides reproduce? Is there some task life enables us to accomplish that being an inanimate, or dead, object does not?

Do not assume being alive is always greater than not. The child never born has it far better than the child born into desolation. I've, at times, often wished that my own existence could be as simple as a rock. Rocks do not know pain, rocks cannot be murdered, rocks do not become frustrated with depression or the state of their existence. To be honest, I'm sure there are many people in the world who would become immensely jealous of rocks if they considered the sum of their existence.

If all life became deceased over night then who would be here to cry for us tomorrow? What suffering would there be if there were no sentient beings alive to perceive such a loss? I can assure you, rocks will not shed any tears for us. So again I ask, what is the purpose of evolution because I do not equate being sentient to being *greater than*. If evolution's only purpose is to ensure the continuation of life, then what difference does it make if we're alive or not? It's kind of funny when you think about it—rocks can hurt us but we can't hurt rocks, so who has the advantage?

I guess you could say, that in the end, we are alive because the process of nature has seen fit for us to be alive, no matter if we appreciate that or not. We live and continue to live because it is natural for us to live. To search for any deeper meaning in life is folly and is to assume that just because there is an event there must be an associated purpose. So I guess religion is neither a mistake nor is it essential to life. Or is it?

Ralph Waldo Emerson once wrote, "Do not the eyes of an embryo predict the light?" Now think, not a single lasting human culture has gone without developing a belief in a supreme being. And not only do we carry a belief, but we also possess a natural drive to be reconnected with such an entity. It is not enough for us to believe but we yearn to be embraced by that which is unseen.

Logic betrays us because of its complete reliance on our senses. To assume everything we can sense is all there is in existence is the greatest mistake any person of *logic* could ever make. We are limited to our ability to perceive. We believe that all that is not perceived is invalid, when in truth, the issue of all that is not perceived should not even be approached because we cannot speak knowledgeably on the subject. But yet, we find a way to speak as if we *know* God. How can we know something that is incapable of being perceived? The answer is, we cannot, but who is to say that we do not perceive God?

Based on the theory of evolution I would assume there was a time in which no creature could see, feel, taste, hear or smell the world around them. It took time to evolve the necessary tools to adapt these senses. We now have eyes, ears, nostrils, hands and tongues to perceive the world, but there was a time when we possessed none of these things. We acknowledge five different methods to perceive the world but what if there was a sixth that we have yet to recognize? What if we could *see* God? What if there was a God sense?

We are the most evolved creatures on the face of the planet due to our minds. Is it difficult to believe that we have adapted, yet, another sense to perceive the world? Is it difficult to believe that there are more ways to experience the universe than the ones we have already discovered? Is it too farfetched to imagine a sense that is a direct product of our evolved human minds?

Our known five senses are the tools we use for communicating with and understanding the world around us. But what if, with the evolution of the human mind, we began to develop another tool for communicating with and understanding the world in which we live? Our eyes sense light, our ears sense sound, our nostrils detect odors and this *God sense* detects God.

I believe we are the only creatures on this earth that wonder about our existence. We have adapted the ability to ask the question *why*. Why are we here? Where did we come from? What is our purpose? I believe that no other creatures on Earth are vexed with such contemplation, and once again, we can contribute this thought process to our human mind and what I consider the soul.

I do not recognize the soul as spiritual essence that transmigrates the body after death. I believe the soul is that sixth sense and the presence of a soul is reflected in the initiative of a being to ask the question *why*. The soul has adapted the ability to experience the presence of a force that was initially beyond our comprehension and awareness. As light is to the eye; God is to the soul.

That is why we have religion; that is why humanity has this naturally recurring drive to search for something that remains *unseen*, but yet, we feel its unrelenting pull on our souls. I am sure that even if I had not been taught religion I would have developed some sort of belief in God because history has proven to us that it is a distinct and natural trait of being human. It is curiosity; we cannot help but wonder what is the source of this *light*. Religion is merely a reflection of the presence of our sixth sense. Faith is like a set of glasses for the soul. It is meant to improve our sight of this Eternal entity that disturbs us from within.

I am convinced that the more science discovers of the world, universe and existence we find ourselves in, the more our discoveries will point us back to the mystery of within. But is this believable? Out of all things we know to exist in this universe, out of all things we have yet to discover, is the whole point meant for us to detect this *light* and follow it back home? We are less than a speck in comparison to the whole of existence and this does not even include the thought of multiple universes existing beyond the perception of our own.

Does it not seem excessive, the scope of all that is known, if the point for us being alive is to discover God? Why would God have created all these other things? Assuming that our universe is not alone, why would God have created those other universes if they do not directly effect our ability to fulfill our purpose which is to detect and follow the light? What is the point of all these stars, galaxies and mysteries that abound if it is all irrelevant to our purpose of discovering God? And let's not forget that these questions are asked under the assumption that there is a God to be discovered in the first place. But I guess all these thoughts also beg the question that God is a sentient being.

What if God is not a sentient being? What if God is not a personae, but more or less, a force that becomes personalized when interwoven with the human mind? What if God did not *decide* to create life but rather it is in God's *nature* to create life? What if our existence, and all that is in the universe, was the result of the creative principle of this *Force?* We could be the product of a force that enabled life, is the source of life and ultimately, the destination of all life.

What if it is true? What if we have created religion and the concept of God, due to our evolved minds, because this *force* has created us? What if our faith truly is the response to this *light* that we have adapted the ability to sense? What if those souls we consider virtuous and upright in their actions and wisdom, are thought to be so because they most accurately reflect the nature of this force we call *God?* That would make the characteristics, and traits we attribute to God, an observed description of the nature of this unseen force. And if we were to label the nature of this force there is one, and only one, word that would accurately describe the nature of God and that is Love.

God is Love. Humans have known this for a long time so there is nothing new about this revelation. God is the complete, unabridged embodiment of the quintessential form of Love. What better description could we attribute to God than Love? That is to assume God actually exist.

As I've said before, it is impossible to prove the existence of God in our current state. All we can do is point to the effect faith has on us. We can point to the belief systems and all the religions which exist throughout the world. We can point to all the mythological tales throughout history that utilize the characters of gods. And once again, we can point to the fact that all human cultures have adapted a belief in God with no exceptions.

The concept of God is like romantic love. You cannot prove love actually exist; it's an intangible concept. All you can do is point to the effects romantic love has on individuals who become partners. When the claim is made that someone is in love it is not because they are located in a box titled *love*. We recognize love by the way people act around one another. We recognize love by the way we feel about another. All that we know about love are the actions, thoughts and emotions it inspires within us. The exact same can be said of God.

As natural as it is for the branches of a tree to reach out towards the light of the sun, it is also natural for the soul of man to reach out towards the *force* that is Love. You can no more deny the existence of faith as you could deny when you are in love. And how can anyone deny that humanity has sought the mysteries of God for as long as it has held the capacity to do so?

In a final word I must say that if we were to ever discover other intelligent life in this universe, or others, if humanity were to ever create artificial intelligence and manifest another sentient being by our own hands then I can guarantee you this—they will have a soul, they will ask *why*, they will *believe*. Because all of nature testifies to the existence of the great force which lives within us—Love

Book of Wine

   The Book of Wine is a collection of quotes that come from the Hindu text *Bhagavad Gita;* the Daoist text Dao de Jing; the sayings of Buddha known as the *Dhammapada;* words from the canonized Gospels of Mark, Luke, Matthew and John; also the gnostic Gospel of Thomas; words from the *Tanakh* which is the Jewish Bible; the *Qu'ran* and *Haddiths* which are the sayings of the Islamic prophet Mohammed; poetry from Rumi who was a Sufi poet which is a branch of Islam; the *Apology of Socrates* who was an ancient Greek philosopher; and also, words from the essays of Ralph Waldo Emerson an American poet and philosopher.

   When I finally discovered what I was looking for in 2006 I found a striking similarity between the above works and my own fresh viewpoint of life. I began to study these works and found that, even though they were written at various times throughout history and in diverse cultures, a single pervading voice could be heard speaking through the different tongues. The same message was coming through all of them and it consistently, unveiled, the truth behind our origins—purpose and destination.

Nothing I have said in this book has not been said before in one form or another. Everything spoken in *Echoes of a Whisper* has been known for a long, long time. The *Book of Wine* is meant to reflect the fact that, even though it has come during various periods of history and from a diverse collection of locales, there exist a single, reliable message that has yet to be successfully contradicted by our knowledge of the world today.

A man gives one coin to be spent among four people. The Persian says, "I want angur." The Arab says, "Inab, you rascal." The Turk, "Uzum!" The Greek, "Shut up all of you. We'll have istafil." They begin pushing each other, then hitting with fists, no stopping it. If a many-languaged master had been there, he could have made peace and told them, "I can give each of you the grapes you want with this one coin. Trust me. Keep quiet, and you four enemies will agree. I also know a silent inner meaning that makes of your four words one wine."

Rumi

Scarcely one out of thousands of persons strives for perfection of Self-realization. Scarcely any one of the striving, or even the perfected persons, truly understands Me.

Bhagavad Gita

Small is the gate and narrow the road that leads to life, and only a few find it.

Gospel of Matthew

I came to this earth so that I can find
the way back to my Beloved.
Rumi

I regard the wise as My very Self, because the one who is
steadfast becomes one with the Supreme Being.
After many births the wise ones resort to Me by
realizing that everything is Brahman (Supreme Being)
indeed. Such a great soul is very rare.
Bhagavad Gita

One day your heart will take you to your lover. One day
your soul will carry you to the Beloved. Don't get lost
in your pain, know that one day
your pain will become your cure.
Rumi

What you are looking forward to has come,
but you don't know it.
Gospel of Thomas

Common souls pay with what they do;
nobler souls with that which they are
Ralph Waldo Emerson

Those that know all, but are lacking in themselves,
are utterly lacking.
Gospel of Thomas

The true poem is the poet's mind;
the true ship is the ship-builder.
Ralph Waldo Emerson

To a Self-realized person the Vedas (scriptures) are as
useful as a reservoir of water when there
is flood water available everywhere.
Bhagavad Gita

When we have broken our god of tradition, and ceased
from our god of rhetoric, then may
God fire the heart with his presence.
Ralph Waldo Emerson

When your intellect, that is confused by the conflicting
opinions and the ritualistic doctrine of the Vedas,
shall stay steady and firm with the Self,
then you shall attain Self-realization.
Bhagavad Gita

If one is whole, one will be filled with light, but if one is
divided one will be filled with darkness.
Gospel of Thomas

You are the candle that lights the whole world and I am
an empty vessel for your light.
Rumi

The spirit of man is YHWH's lamp;
it searches out his inmost being.
Proverbs

God is the light of the heavens and earth. His light is like a niche in which is a lamp-the lamp encased in glass-the glass, as it were, a glistening star. From a blessed tree it is lighted, the olive, neither of the East nor of the West, whose oil appears to give light even though f ire does not touch it. It is light upon light. God guides whoever he pleases to His light, and God sets forth parables for men, for God knows all things.
Qur'an

Images are visible to people, but the light within them is hidden in the image of the Father's light. He will be disclosed, but his image is hidden by his light.
Gospel of Thomas

The wise grieve neither for the living nor for the dead. There was never a time when I, you or these kings did not exist; nor shall we ever cease to exist in the future.
Bhagavad Gita

You are a diver; your body is just clothing left at the shore.
Rumi

Seeing your body as no better than an earthen pot, make war on Mara (the devil) with the sword of wisdom, and setting up your mind as a fortress, defend what you have won, remaining free from attachment.
Dhammapada

The Atma (soul) is neither born nor does it die at any
time, nor having been it will cease to exist again. It is
unborn, eternal, permanent, and primeval. The Atma is
not destroyed when the body is destroyed.

Bhagavad Gita

For the fear of death is indeed the pretense of wisdom,
and not real wisdom, being pretense of knowing
the unknown; and no one knows whether death,
which men in their fear apprehend to be the greatest
evil, may not be the greatest good.

Socrates

When you die, death will disclose the mystery-not the
death that takes you into the dark grave, but the
death whereby you are transmuted and enter
into the Light. O Amir, wield the mace against yourself:
shatter egoism to pieces!

Rumi

Though one were to defeat thousands upon thousands
of men in battle, if another were to overcome just
one-himself, he is the supreme victor.

Dhammapada

The Atma is said to be unmanifest, unthinkable, and
unchanging. Knowing this Atma as such you should not
grieve...because, death is certain for the one who is born,
and birth is certain for the one who dies. Therefore,
you should not lament over the inevitable.

Bhagavad Gita

A lover love's death, which is God's way of helping us evolve from mineral to vegetable to animal, the one incorporating the others. Then animal becomes Adam, and the next will take us beyond what we can imagine, into the mystery of we are returning. Don't fear death. Spill your jug in the river! Your attributes disappear, but the essence moves on. Your shame and fear are like felt layers covering coldness. Throw them off, and rush naked into the joy of death.

Rumi

A man that is good for anything ought not calculate the chance of living or dying; he ought only to consider whether in doing anything he is doing right or wrong-acting the part of a good man or of a bad.

Socrates

When people are born, they are tender and supple. At death they are stiff and hard. All things, like plants and trees, are tender and pliant while alive. At death they are dried and withered. Therefore the stiff and hard are companions of death. The tender and supple are companions of life. Thus the strong arms do not win. A stiff tree will break, the hard and strong will fall. The tender and supple will rise.

Dao De Jing

I died as mineral and became a plant, I died as plant and rose to animal, I died as animal and I was Man. Why should I fear? When was I less by dying? Yet once more I shall die as Man, to soar with angels blest; but even from angelhood I must pass on: all except God doth perish. When I have sacrificed my angel-soul, I shall

become what no mind e'er conceived. Oh, let me not
exist! For Non-existence proclaims in organ tones.
"To him we shall return."
Rumi

The hour of departure has arrived, and we go our ways-I
to die, and you to live. Which is better God only knows.
Socrates

O Arjuna, I am the Atma abiding in the heart of all
beings. I am also the beginning, the middle, and
the end of all beings.
Bhagavad Gita

If you look deep in your heart you will find Him within
yourself...there is some merit in the suffering you have
endured, but what a pity you have not discovered
the Mecca that's inside.
Rumi

He has also set eternity in the hearts of men; yet they
cannot fathom what God has done from beginning to end.
Ecclesiastes

You are only an instrument, O Arjuna.
Bhagavad Gita

We lie in the lap of immense intelligence, which makes us receivers of its truth and organs of its activity. When we discern justice, when we discern truth, we do nothing of ourselves, but allow a passage to its beams. If we ask whence this comes, if we seek to pry into the soul that causes, all philosophy is at fault. Its presence or its absence is all we can affirm.

Ralph Waldo Emerson

The Lord abides in the heart of all beings, O Arjuna, causing all beings to act by His power of Maya as if they are mounted on a machine.

Bhahavad Gita

All goes to show that the soul in man is not an organ, but animates and exercises all the organs; is not a function, like the power of memory, of calculation, of comparison, but uses these as hands and feet; is not a faculty, but a light; is not the intellect or the will, but the master of the intellect and the will; is the background of our being, in which they lie,-an immensity not possessed and that cannot be possessed. From within or from behind, a light shines through us upon things, and makes us aware that we are nothing, but the light is all. A man is the fasade of a temple wherein all wisdom and all good abide.

Ralph Waldo Emerson

Deafened by the voice of desire you are unaware the Beloved lives in the core of your heart. Stop the noise and you will hear His voice in the silence.

Rumi

The crucible for silver and the furnace for gold,
but YHWH tests the heart.
Proverbs

Atma in the body is My eternal
indivisible fragment indeed.
Bhahavad Gita

Be not like those who forget God, therefore
He caused them to forget their own souls.
Qur'an

You are searching the world for treasure but the real
treasure is yourself. If you are tempted by bread you will
find only bread. What you seek for you become.
Rumi

Those who have found themselves,
of them the world is not worthy.
Gospel of Thomas

O Friend, you made me lovingly, You clothed me in a
robe of skin and blood then planted deep inside me a
seed from Your heart. You turned the whole world into
a sanctuary where You are the only One.
Rumi

When you know yourselves, then you will be known, and
you will understand that you are children of the living
Father. But if you do not know yourselves, then you live
in poverty, and you are the poverty.
Gospel of Thomas

Until you know yourself you will be distant from God.
Rumi

Whoever is near me is near the fire, and whoever is far
from me is far from the Father's kingdom.
Gospel of Thomas

By doing his own work, he unfolds himself.
Ralph Waldo Emerson

One attains the highest perfection by devotion to one's
natural work. Listen to Me how one attains perfection
while engaged in natural work. He from whom all beings
originate, and by whom all this universe is pervaded;
worshiping him by performing one's natural duty for
Him one attains perfection. One's inferior natural work
is better than superior unnatural work. One who does the
work ordained by one's inherent nature incurs no sin.
Bhagavad Gita

That which each can do best, none but his
Maker can teach him.
Ralph Waldo Emerson

But to those who worship Me as the personal God, re-
nouncing all actions to Me; setting Me as their supreme
goal, and meditating on me with single-minded devotion;
I swiftly become their savior, from the world that is the
ocean of death and transmigration,
whose thoughts are set on Me, O Arjuna.
Bhagavad Gita

For know that this is the command of God; and I
believe that no greater good has ever happened in the
state than my service to the God. For I do nothing but
go about persuading you all, old and young alike, not
to take thought for your persons of your properties,
but first chiefly to care about the greatest improvement of the soul. I tell you that virtue is not given by
money, but that from virtue comes money and every
other good of man, public as well as private. This is
my teaching, and if this is the doctrine which corrupts
the youth, I am a mischievous person.
Socrates

When a man believes in me, he does not believe in me
only, but in the one who sent me. When he looks
at me, he sees the one who sent me. I have come
into the world as a light, so that no one who believes
in me should stay in darkness.
Gospel of John

Whoever sees me has seen truth.
Hadiths

When a fly is plunged in honey, all the members of its
body are reduced to the same condition, and it does not
move. Similarly the term *istighraq* (absorption in God) is
applied to one who had no conscious existence or initiative or movement. Any action that proceeds from him is
not his own. If he is still struggling in the water, or if he
cries out, "Oh, I am drowning," he is not said to be in the
state of absorption. This is what is signified by the words
Ana 'l-Haqq "I am God." People imagine that it is a
presumptuous claim, whereas it is really a presumptuous

claim to say *Ana 'l-abd* "I am the slave of God"; and *Ana 'l-Haqq* "I am God" is an expression of great humility. The man who says *Ana 'l-abd* "I am the slave of God" affirms two existences, his own and God's, but he that says *Ana 'l-Haqq* "I am God" has made himself non-existent and has given himself up and says "I am God," i.e. "I am naught, He is all: there is no being but God's." this is the extreme of humility and self-abasement.

Rumi

But prayer as a means to effect a private end is meanness and theft. It supposes dualism and not unity in nature and consciousness. As soon as the man is at one with God, he will not beg. He will then see prayer in all action. The prayer of the farmer kneeling in his field to weed it, the prayer of the rower kneeling with the stroke of his oar, are true prayers heard throughout nature, though for cheap ends.

Ralph Waldo Emerson

Ineffable is the union of man and God in every act of the soul. The simplest person, who in his integrity worships God, becomes God; yet for ever and ever the influx of this better and universal self is new and unsearchable.

Ralph Waldo Emerson

If you really have known me, you will know my Father as well. From now on, you do know him and have seen him.

Gospel of John

We know better than we do. We do not yet possess ourselves, and we know at the same time that we are much
more. I feel the same truth how often in my trivial conversation with my neighbours, that somewhat higher in
each of us overlooks this by-play, and Jove
nods to Jove from behind each of us.
Ralph Waldo Emerson

There is a tree in India. If you eat the fruit of that tree,
you'll never grow old and never die...My son, this is not
an actual tree, though it's been called that. Sometimes
it's called a sun, sometimes an ocean, or a cloud. These
words point to the wisdom that comes through a true
human being, which may have many effects, the least of
which is eternal life! In the same way one person can be
a father to you and a son to someone else, uncle to another and nephew to yet another, so what you are looking for
has many names, and one existence. Don't search for one
of the names. Move beyond any attachment to names.
Rumi

The Supreme Spirit in the body is also called the witness,
the guide, the supporter, the enjoyer, and the great Lord...
some perceive God in the heart by the intellect through
meditation; others by the yoga of knowledge;
and others by the yoga of work. Some, however,
do not understand Brahman, but having heard from
others, take to worship. They also transcend death by
their firm faith to what they have heard.
Bhagavad Gita

I will ask the Father, and he will give you another Counselor to be with you forever-the Spirit of truth. The world
cannot accept him, because it neither sees him
nor knows him. But you know him, for he
lives with you and is in you.
Gospel of John

When it breathes through his intellect, it is genius; when
it breathes through his will, it is virtue; when it flows
through his affection, it is love.
Ralph Waldo Emerson

If the flesh came into being because of spirit, that is a
marvel, but if spirit came into being because of the body,
that is a marvel of marvels. Yet I marvel at how this great
wealth has come to dwell in this poverty.
Gospel of Thomas

If this me is only a robe then
who is the one I am covering?
Rumi

When you see your likeness, you are happy. But when
you see your images that came into being before you and
that neither die nor become visible,
how much you will have to bear!
Gospel of Thomas

What is praised is one, so the praise is one too, many
jugs being poured into a huge basin. All religions, all this
singing, one song. The differences are just illusion and
vanity. Sunlight looks slightly different on this wall than
it does on that wall and a lot different on this other one,

but it is still one light. We have borrowed these clothes,
these time-and-space personalities, from a light, and
when we praise, we pour them back in.
Rumi

Whoever drinks from my mouth will become like me;
I myself shall become that person, and the
hidden things will be revealed to him.
Gospel of Thomas

We are wiser than we know. If we will not interfere with
our thought, but will act entirely, or see how the thing
stands in God, we know the particular thing, and every
thing, and every man. For the Maker of all things and all
persons stands behind us, and casts his dread
omniscience through us over things.
Ralph Waldo Emerson

We created man; and We know what his soul whispers
within him, and We are nearer to him
than his jugular vein.
Qur'an

My love, you are closer to me than myself,
you shine through my eyes.
Rumi

If you do not fast from the world, you will
not find the kingdom.
Gospel of Thomas

Look on the world as a bubble, look on it as a mirage.
The King of Death never finds him who
views the world like that.
Dhammapada

Whoever has come to know the world has discovered a
carcass, and whoever has discovered a carcass,
of that person the world is not worthy.
Gospel of Thomas

Be in the world as if you were a stranger or a traveler.
Hadiths

Be passersby
Gospel of Thomas

Your wealth and your children are only a source of trial,
but with God is the great reward.
Qur'an

Therefore the wise put themselves last, but find themselves foremost. They exclude themselves, and yet they
always remain. Is it not because they do not live for
themselves that they find themselves fulfilled?
Dao De Jing

He has no need for faith who knows the uncreated, who
has cut off rebirth, who has destroyed any opportunity
for good or evil, and cast away all desire.
He is indeed the ultimate man.
Dhammapada

Those who know others are wise. Those who know
themselves are enlightened. Those who overcome others
require force. Those who overcome themselves
need strength. Those who are content are wealthy.
Those who persevere have will power. Those who
do not lose their center endure. Those who die
but maintain their power live eternally.
Dao De Jing

Love your enemies and pray for those who persecute
you, that you may be sons of your Father in heaven...be
perfect, therefore, as your heavenly Father is perfect.
Gospel of Matthew

When the wise hear the Way, they practice it diligently.
When the mediocre hear of the Way, they doubt it. When
the foolish hear of the Way, they laugh out loud.
If it were not laughed at, it would not be the Way.
Dao De Jing

One is not a learned man by virtue of much speaking...
one is not a bearer of the teaching by virtue of much
speaking, but he who, even if he has only studied a little,
has experienced the truth in person, he is indeed a bearer
of the teaching, who has not forgotten the teaching.
Dhammapada

Therefore those who value the world as themselves may
be entrusted to govern the world. Those who love
the world as themselves may be entrusted
to care for the world.
Dao De Jing

It is not the shortcoming of others, nor what others have
done or not done that one should think about, but what
one has done or not done oneself.
Dhammapada

None of you has faith unless he loves for his brother
what he loves for himself.
Hadiths

Those who know do not speak. Those who speak
do not know...those achieving it are detached from
friends and enemies, from benefit and harm,
from honor and disgrace. Therefore they are
the most valuable people in the world.
Dao De Jing

The soul is the perceiver and revealer of truth. We know
truth when we see it, let skeptic and scoffer say what they
choose. Foolish people ask you, when you have spoken
what they do not wish to hear, 'How do you know it is
truth, and not an error of your own?'
We know truth when we see it, from opinion,
as we know when we are awake that we are awake.
Ralph Waldo Emerson

Careful amidst the careless, amongst the sleeping
wide-awake, the intelligent man leaves them all behind,
like a race-horse does a mere hack.
Dhammapada

I took my stand in the midst of the world, and in flesh I
appeared to them. I found them all drunk, and I did not
find any of them thirsty. My soul ached for the children

of humanity, because they are blind in their hearts and do not see, for they came into the world empty, and they also seek to depart from the world empty. But meanwhile they are drunk. When they shake off their wine, then they will change their ways.

Gospel of Thomas

Those of you who feel no love, sleep on. Those of you who do not feel the sorrow of love in whose heart passion has never risen, sleep on. Those who do not long for union who are not constantly asking, "Where is He?," sleep on. Love's path is outside of all religious sects if trickery and hypocrisy is your way, sleep on.
If you don't melt like copper in your quest for the alchemical gold, sleep on. If like a drunkard you fall left and right unaware the night has passed and it's time for prayer, sleep on. Fate has taken my sleep but since it has not taken yours, young man, sleep on. We have fallen into love's hands, since you are in your own, sleep on. I am the one who is drunk on Love, since you are drunk on food, sleep on. I have given up my head and have nothing more to say, but you can wrap yourself in the robe of words and sleep on.

Rumi

For if you kill me you will not easily find a successor to me, who, if I may use such a ludicrous figure of speech, I am a sort of gadfly, given to the state by God; and the state is a great and noble steed who is tardy in his motions owing to his very size, and requires to be stirred into life. I am that gadfly which God has attached to the state, and all day long and in all places am always fastening upon you, arousing and persuading and reproaching

you. You will not easily find another like me, and therefore I would advise you to spare me. I dare say that you
may feel out of temper (like a person who is suddenly
awakened from sleep), and you think that you might
easily strike me dead as Anytus advises, and then you
would sleep on for the remainder of your lives, unless
God in his care of you sent another gadfly. When I say
that I am given to you by God, the proof of my mission
is this:-if I had been like other men, I should not have
neglected all my own concerns or patiently seen the
neglect of them during all these years, and have been
doing yours, coming to you individually like a father
or elder brother, exhorting you to regard virtue; such
conduct, I say, would be unlike human nature.
If I had gained anything, or if my exhortations had
been paid, there would have been some sense in my
doing so; but now, as you will perceive, not even
the impudence of my accusers dares to say that
I have ever exacted or sought pay of any one;
of that they have no witness. And I have a sufficient
witness to the truth of what I say-my poverty.

Socrates

Sheikh Sarrazi wants only intimacy with the voice he
hears. Love for the invisible is enough. He needs no
wages. There is nourishment like bread that feeds one
part of your life and nourishment like light for another.
There are many rules about restraint with the former, but
only one rule for the latter, Never be satisfied. Eat and
drink the soul substance, as a wick does with the oil it
soaks in. Give light to the company.

Rumi

I tell you the truth, no one can enter the kingdom of God unless he is born of water and the Spirit. Flesh gives birth to flesh, but the Spirit gives birth to spirit. You should not be surprised at my saying, 'You must be born again.' The wind blows wherever it pleases. You hear its sound, but you cannot tell where it comes from or where it is going. So it is with everyone born of the Spirit.

Gospel of John

The best are like water. Water benefits all things, and does not compete with them. It flows to the lowest level that people disdain. In this it comes near to the Way.

Dao De Jing

Now this duty of cross-examining other men had been imposed upon me by God; and has been signified to me by oracles, visions, and in every way in which the will of divine power was ever intimated to any one.

Socrates

If God were your Father, you would love me,
for I came from God and now am here.
I have not come on my own; but he sent me.

Gospel of John

For the word which I will speak is not mine. I will refer you to a witness who is worthy of credit; that witness shall be the God of Delphi—he will tell you about my wisdom, if I have any, and of what sort it is.

Socrates

Those who see me in everything and see everything in Me, are not separated from Me and I am not separated from them...one is considered to be the best yogi who regards every being like oneself, and who can feel the pain and pleasures of others as one's own, O Arjuna.
Bhagavad Gita

Believe me when I say that I am in the Father and the Father is in me.
Gospel of John

God has declared: I am close to the thought that My servant has of Me, and I am with him wherever he recollects Me. If he remembers Me in himself, I remember him in Myself, and if he remembers Me in a gathering, I remember him better than those in the gathering do, and if he approaches Me by as much as one hand's length, I approach him by a cubit...If he takes a step towards Me, I run towards him.
Hadiths

The Self is present equally in all beings. There is no one hateful or dear to Me. But, those who worship Me with devotion, they are with Me and I am also with them. Even if the most sinful person resolves to worship Me with single-minded loving devotion, such a person must be regarded as a saint because of making the right resolution. Such a person soon becomes righteous and attains everlasting peace. Be aware, O Arjuna, that My devotee never falls down. Anybody, including women, merchants, laborers, and the evil-minded can attain the supreme goal by just surrendering unto My will, O Arjuna.
Bhagavad Gita

Therefore embrace the One and become examples
for the world...is not the ancient saying true,
"To yield is to preserve unity?" for true wholeness
comes from turning within.
Dao De Jing

A person is said to have achieved yoga, the union with
the Self, when the perfectly disciplined mind gets free-
dom from all desires, and becomes absorbed in the Self
alone. As a lamp in a spot sheltered from the wind does
not flicker, this simile is used for the subdued mind
of a yogi practicing meditation on Brahman.
Bhagavad Gita

The ancients attained oneness.
Dao De Jing

I am the captive of this journey. It is the scent of home
that keeps me going, the hope of union, the face of my
Beloved. I know our fate is separation, but until my
last breath I will search for my sweet love,
I will seek my home.
Rumi

A large country is like low land where rivers flow, a
place where everything comes together, the female of all.
The female overcomes the male with tranquility.
Tranquility is underneath.
Dao De Jing

Fix your mind on Me, be devoted to Me, worship Me,
and bow down to Me. Thus uniting yourself with Me,
and setting Me as the supreme goal and sole refuge, you
shall certainly realize Me.
Bhagavad Gita

Being the valley of the world is eternal power and returning to the innocence of a baby...being an example for the
world is eternal power and returning to the infinite.
Dao De Jing

I was absorbed in my work in this world but I never
lost my longing for home. One day, exhausted with no
strength left, I was lifted suddenly by the grace of Love.
To describe this mystery there are no words.
Rumi

Empty yourself of everything. Maintain a steady serenity.
All things take shape and become active,
but I see them return to their source.
Dao De Jing

Therefore the wise say, "Those who bear the humiliation
of the people are able to minister to them. Those who
take upon themselves the sins of the society are able to
lead the world." Words of truth seem so paradoxical.
Dao De Jing

I am the origin of all. Everything emanates from Me.
Understanding this, the wise ones worship Me with love
and devotion. With their minds absorbed in Me, with
their lives surrendered unto Me, always enlightening
each other by talking about Me; they remain ever content

and delighted. I give the knowledge, to those who are ever united with Me and lovingly adore Me, by which they come to Me. Out of compassion for them I, who dwell within their heart, destroy the darkness born of ignorance by the shining lamp of knowledge.
Bhagavad Gita

Why did the ancients prize this Way? Did they not say, "Seek, and you will find; let go, and you will be forgiven." Therefore the Way is valued by the world.
Dao De Jing

Those who seek should not stop seeking until they find. When they find, they will be disturbed. When they are disturbed, they will marvel, and will reign over all. And after they have reigned they will rest.
Gospel of Thomas

This unmanifest state is called the imperishable or Brahman. This is said to be the ultimate goal. Those who reach My Supreme abode do not return. This Supreme abode, O Arjuna, is attainable by unswerving devotion to Me within which all beings exist, and by which all this universe is pervaded.
Bhagavad Gita

The Way that can be described is not the absolute Way; the name that can be given is not the absolute name. Nameless it is the source of heaven and earth; named it is the mother of all things. Whoever is desireless, sees the essence of life. Whoever desires, sees its manifestations.
Dao De Jing

Arjuna said, "Those ever-steadfast devotees who thus worship You and those who worship the eternal unmanifest Brahman, which of these has the best knowledge of yoga?" The Supreme Lord said, "Those ever steadfast devotees who worship with supreme faith by fixing their mind on me as personal God, I consider them to be the best yogis. But those who worship the imperishable, the undefinable, the unmanifest, the omnipresent, the unthinkable, the unchanging, the immovable, and the eternal Brahman; restraining all the senses, even minded under all circumstances, engaged in the welfare of all creatures, they also attain Me. Self-realization is more difficult for those who fix their mind on the formless Brahman, because the comprehension of the unmanifest Brahman by the average embodied human being is very difficult."

Bhagavad Gita

The Way is infinite, its use is never exhausted. It is bottomless, like the fountainhead of all things...deep and still, ever present. I do not know its source. It seems to have existed before the Lord.

Dao De Jing

Everyone who drinks this water will be thirsty again, but whoever drinks the water I give him will never thirst. Indeed, the water I give him will become in him a spring of water welling up to eternal life.

Gospel of John

While the mind sees only boundaries, Love knows the secret way there. While the mind smells profit and quickly sets up shop, Love sees untold of treasures far beyond. Lovers trust in the wealth of their hearts, while the all-knowing mind sees only thorns ahead.
Rumi

The great Way flows everywhere, both left and right. All things derive their life from it, and it does not turn away from them. It accomplishes its work, but does not take possession. It provides for and nourishes everything, but does not control them. Always without desires, it may be considered small. The destination of all things, yet claiming nothing.
Dao De Jing

The kingdom of heaven is like a mustard seed, which a man took and planted in his field. Though it is the smallest of all your seeds, yet when it grows, it is the largest of garden plants and becomes a tree, so that the birds of the air come and perch in its branches.
Gospel of Matthew

I continually support the entire universe by a small fraction of My energy.
Bhagavad Gita

The kingdom of heaven is like yeast that a woman took and mixed into a large amount of flour until it worked all through the dough.
Gospel of Matthew

Arjuna saw the entire universe, divided in many ways,
but standing as One in the body of Krishna,
the God of gods.
Bhagavad Gita

We know the authentic effects of the true fire through
every one of its million disguises.
Ralph Waldo Emerson

There is something mysterious and whole which existed
before heaven and earth, silent, formless, complete, and
never changing. Living eternally everywhere in
perfection, it is the mother of all things. I do not know
its name; I call it the Way. If forced to define it,
I shall call it supreme. Supreme means absolute.
Absolute means extending everywhere. Extending
everywhere means returning to itself.
Dao De Jing

I know where I come from and where I am going.
But you have no idea where I come from
or where I am going.
Gospel of John

Returning to the source is serenity; it is to realize one's
destiny. To realize one's destiny is to know the eternal.
To know the eternal is to be enlightened.
Not to know the eternal is to act blindly
and court disaster.
Dao De Jing

After Self-Realization, one does not regard any other
gain superior to Self-Realization. Established in
Self-Realization, one is not moved even
by the greatest calamity.
Bhagavad Gita

It will not come by watching for it. It will not be said,
'Look, here!' or 'Look, there!' Rather, the Father's
kingdom is spread out upon the earth,
and people don't see it.
Gospel of Thomas

When one perceives the diverse variety of beings resting
in One and spreading out from That alone, then one
attains Brahman...O Arjuna, just as one sun illuminates
this entire world, similarly the Creator illumines
the entire creation.
Bhagavad Gita

If your leaders say to you, 'Look the kingdom is in the
sky,' then the birds of the sky will precede you.
If they say to you, 'It is in the sea,' then the fish
will precede you. Rather, the kingdom is within
you and it is outside you.
Gospel of Thomas

Meet it, and you do not see its beginning.
Follow it, and you do not see its end.
Dao De Jing

Great power appears like a valley. Great purity appears
tarnished. Great character appears insufficient.
Solid character appears weak. True integrity appears
changeable. Great space has no corners. Great
ability takes time to mature. Great music has
the subtlest sound. Great form has no shape.
Dao De Jing

All by itself the soil produces grain-first the stalk, then
the head, then the full kernel in the head. As soon as
the grain is ripe, he puts the sickle to it,
because the harvest has come.
Gospel of Mark

The Way never interferes, yet through
it everything is done.
Dao De Jing

It takes a thousand stages for the perfect being to
evolve. Every step of the way I will walk with
you and never leave you stranded. Be patient, do not
open the lid too soon, simmer away
until you are ready.
Rumi

When the crop ripened, he came quickly
carrying a sickle and harvested it.
Gospel of Thomas

God exists. There is a soul at the centre of nature, and over the will of every man, so that none of us can wrong the universe. It has so infused its strong enchantment into nature, that we prosper when we accept its advice.
Ralph Waldo Emerson

The Way of heaven does not strive; yet it wins easily. It does not speak; yet it gets a good response. It does not demand; yet all needs are met. It is not anxious; yet it plans well. The net of heaven is vast; its meshes are wide, but nothing slips through.
Dao De Jing

That Unity, that Over-soul, within which every man's particular being is contained and made one with all other; that common heart, of which all sincere conversation is worship, to which all right action is submission...within man is the soul of the whole...the eternal ONE.
Ralph Waldo Emerson

O Creator and Lord of all beings, God of all gods,
Supreme person and Lord of the universe,
You alone know Yourself by Yourself.
Bhagavad Gita

Again, the kingdom of heaven is like a merchant looking for fine pearls. When he found one of great value, he went away and sold everything he had and bought it.
Gospel of Matthew

The one that does not love does not know God,
for God is Love
First Letter of John

The minute I heard my first love story I started
looking for you, not knowing how blind that was.
Lovers don't finally meet somewhere.
They're in each other all along.
Rumi

Credits

The quotes found in *Book of Wine* come from the sources which follows. You can learn more about these sources at www.cbhproducts.com

1. *Bhagavad Gita*

2. *Dao de Jing*

3. *Proverbs* of the Biblical Old Testament

4. *Ecclesiastes* of the Biblical Old Testament

5. *Dhammapada*

6. *The Apology of Socrates*

7. *Gospels of Matthew, Mark, Luke and John* of the Biblical New Testament

8. *Gospel of Thomas* of the Gnostic Gospels

9. *First Letter of John* of the Biblical New Testament

10. *Qu'ran*

11. *Jesus and Muhammad: The Parrallel Sayings* edited by Joey Green

12. *The Soul of Rumi* translated by Coleman Barks

13. *Rumi: Hidden Music* translated by Maryam Mafi & Azima Melita Kolin

14. *Rumi* edited by Peter Washington

15. *Spiritual Laws* essay of Ralph Waldo Emerson

16. *The Over-Soul* essay of Ralph Waldo Emerson

17. *History* essay of Ralph Waldo Emerson

18. *Self-Reliance* essay of Ralph Waldo Emerson

Made in the USA
Columbia, SC
10 September 2023

22676667R00081